·EXPLORING·
SCIENCE AND MEDICAL DISCOVERIES

Antibiotics

·EXPLORING·
SCIENCE AND MEDICAL DISCOVERIES

Antibiotics

Other books in the
Exploring Science and Medical Discoveries series:

Cloning
Gene Therapy
Vaccines

EXPLORING

SCIENCE AND MEDICAL DISCOVERIES

Antibiotics

Lisa Yount, *Book Editor*

Bruce Glassman, *Vice President*
Bonnie Szumski, *Publisher*
Helen Cothran, *Managing Editor*
David M. Haugen, *Series Editor*

GREENHAVEN PRESS
An imprint of Thomson Gale, a part of The Thomson Corporation

Detroit • New York • San Francisco • San Diego • New Haven, Conn.
Waterville, Maine • London • Munich

LIBRARY OF CONGRESS CATALOGING-IN-PUBLICATION DATA

Antibiotics / Lisa Yount, book editor.
    p. cm. — (Exploring science and medical discoveries)
    Includes bibliographical references and index.
    ISBN 0-7377-1961-3 (lib. : alk. paper) — ISBN 0-7377-1962-1 (pbk. : alk. paper)
    1. Antibiotics—Popular works. I. Yount, Lisa. II. Series
RM267.A52   2005
615'.329—dc22
                                                       2004042523

Printed in the United States of America

CONTENTS

Chapter 1: Before Antibiotics

1. A Deadly Epidemic

by Giovanni Boccaccio   26

In 1348 a plague called the Black Death swept through Europe, killing millions of people and creating tremendous social disruption. It was a dramatic example of the damage that bacterial diseases produced before antibiotics were discovered.

2. Microorganisms Cause Disease

by Patrice Debré   34

Around 1877 renowned French chemist Louis Pasteur and German bacteriologist Robert Koch proved that illnesses such as anthrax, a deadly ailment that usually affects sheep and cattle, are caused by bacteria and other microorganisms.

3. Killing Germs in Wounds

by Joseph Lister   45

In the 1860s Joseph Lister, a British surgeon, read about Pasteur's early demonstrations that germs caused decay of meat and guessed that they might cause infections in wounds as well. He discovered that using a chemical called carbolic acid to kill germs in wounds could prevent such infections.

4. Searching for Magic Bullets

by Ernst Bäumler   53

German bacteriologist Paul Ehrlich began searching for what he called "magic bullets"—chemicals that would destroy particular disease-causing microbes inside the body—in the early 1900s.

Chapter 2: The Discovery of Antibiotics

1. Alexander Fleming Discovers Penicillin
In 1928 Scottish bacteriologist Alexander Fleming noticed that bacteria could not grow near a type of mold. Fleming discovered the mold produced a chemical that was later developed into the antibiotic penicillin.

2. Gerhard Domagk Discovers the Sulfa Drugs
German scientist Gerhard Domagk found in 1935 that a red dye called Prontosil killed certain kinds of disease-causing bacteria. His discovery led to development of the sulfa drugs, which were the first drugs that, like antibiotics, destroyed multiple types of bacteria.

3. Penicillin and Luck
Biochemist Norman G. Heatley, a member of Howard Florey's team, worked out several ingenious ways to grow Pencillium mold and harvest penicillin—guided, he claimed, partly by luck. The group then tested the drug on mice, with spectacular results.

4. Selman A. Waksman Discovers Streptomycin
Streptomycin was another successful antibiotic developed in the 1940s. Russian American scientist Selman A. Waksman's long experience with soil microbiology helped him discover this drug in 1943.

Chapter 3: Antibiotics' Golden Age

1. Penicillin's First Miracles
As early as 1942 when it was available only in minute

quantities, penicillin began saving lives. The reputation of penicillin and other antibiotics as "wonder drugs" grew out of these early successes.

Chapter 4: Antibiotics Today: The Threat of Resistance

Most great science and medical discoveries emerge slowly from the work of generations of scientists. In their laboratories, far removed from the public eye, scientists seek cures for human diseases, explore more efficient methods to feed the world's hungry, and develop technologies to improve quality of life. A scientist, trained in the scientific method, may spend his or her entire career doggedly pursuing a goal such as a cure for cancer or the invention of a new drug. In the pursuit of these goals, most scientists are single-minded, rarely thinking about the moral and ethical issues that might arise once their new ideas come into the public view. Indeed, it could be argued that scientific inquiry requires just that type of objectivity.

Moral and ethical assessments of scientific discoveries are quite often made by the unscientific—the public—sometimes for good, sometimes for ill. When a discovery is unveiled to society, intense scrutiny often ensues. The media report on it, politicians debate how it should be regulated, ethicists analyze its impact on society, authors vilify or glorify it, and the public struggles to determine whether the new development is friend or foe. Even without fully understanding the discovery or its potential impact, the public will often demand that further inquiry be stopped. Despite such negative reactions, however, scientists rarely quit their pursuits; they merely find ways around the roadblocks.

Embryonic stem cell research, for example, illustrates this tension between science and public response. Scientists engage in embryonic stem cell research in an effort to treat diseases such as Parkinson's and diabetes that are the result of cellular dysfunction. Embryonic stem cells can be derived from early-stage embryos, or blastocysts, and coaxed to form any kind of human cell or tissue. These can then be used to replace damaged or diseased tissues in those suffering from intractable diseases. Many researchers believe that the use of embryonic stem cells to treat human diseases promises to be one of the most important advancements in medicine.

However, embryonic stem cell experiments are highly contro-versial in the public sphere. At the center of the tumult is the fact that in order to create embryonic stem cell lines, human embryos must be destroyed. Blastocysts often come from fertilized eggs that are left over from fertility treatments. Critics argue that since blas-tocysts have the capacity to grow into human beings, they should be granted the full range of rights given to all humans, including the right not to be experimented on. These analysts contend, there-fore, that destroying embryos is unethical. This argument received attention in the highest office of the United States. President George W. Bush agreed with the critics, and in August 2001 he an-nounced that scientists using federal funds to conduct embryonic stem cell research would be restricted to using existing cell lines. He argued that limiting research to existing lines would prevent any new blastocysts from being destroyed for research.

Scientists have criticized Bush's decision, saying that restrict-ing research to existing cell lines severely limits the number and types of experiments that can be conducted. Despite this consid-erable roadblock, however, scientists quickly set to work trying to figure out a way to continue their valuable research. Unsurpris-ingly, as the regulatory environment in the United States becomes restrictive, advancements occur elsewhere. A good example con-cerns the latest development in the field. On February 12, 2004, professor Hwang Yoon-Young of Hanyang University in Seoul, South Korea, announced that he was the first to clone a human embryo and then extract embryonic stem cells from it. Hwang's research means that scientists may no longer need to use blasto-cysts to perform stem cell research. Scientists around the world extol the achievement as a major step in treating human diseases.

The debate surrounding embryonic stem cell research illustrates the moral and ethical pressure that the public brings to bear on the scientific community. However, while nonexperts often criticize scientists for not considering the potential negative impact of their work, ironically the public's reaction against such discoveries can produce harmful results as well. For example, although the outcry against embryonic stem cell research in the United States has re-sulted in fewer embryos being destroyed, those with Parkinson's, such as actor Michael J. Fox, have argued that prohibiting the de-velopment of new stem cell lines ultimately will prevent a timely cure for the disease that is killing Fox and thousands of others.

Greenhaven Press's Exploring Science and Medical Discoveries series explores the public uproar that often follows the disclosure of scientific advances in fields such as stem cell research. Each anthology traces the history of one major scientific or medical discovery, investigates society's reaction to the breakthrough, and explores potential new applications and avenues of research. Primary sources provide readers with eyewitness accounts of crucial moments in the discovery process, and secondary sources offer historical perspectives on the scientific achievement and society's reaction to it. Volumes also contain useful research tools, including an introductory essay providing important context, and an annotated table of contents enabling students to quickly locate selections of interest. A thorough index helps readers locate content easily, a detailed chronology helps students trace the history of the discovery, and an extensive bibliography guides readers interested in pursuing further research.

Greenhaven Press's Exploring Science and Medical Discoveries series provides readers with inspiring accounts of how generations of scientists made the world's great discoveries possible and investigates the tremendous impact those innovations have had on the world.

The Trouble with Magic Bullets

Around 1905, German microbiologist Paul Ehrlich, inventor of the first deliberately designed drug that successfully killed a specific type of disease-causing microorganism inside the human body, began to speak of drugs as potential "magic bullets" that, like the body's own immune defenses, would "seek out their own target without damaging the organism."[1] Ehrlich's warlike metaphor was to shape, even seemingly to sum up, twentieth-century medicine's attitude toward infectious diseases (those caused by microorganisms).

Early Explanations for Disease

Doctors and patients had not always thought of disease, even infectious disease, as an attack by unseen enemies. Until the late nineteenth century, most people believed that illness resulted from disturbances in the environment, the human body, or both. One common theory claimed that diseases, especially epidemic diseases—those that sprang up suddenly and spread rapidly through an area—were caused by foul-smelling poisons given off by decaying matter such as human and animal corpses. Another widely held belief, popularized by the legendary ancient Greek physician Hippocrates and his equally renowned Roman successor, Galen, stated that disease arose from an imbalance in the humors, four liquids that were thought to circulate throughout the body.

A third proposal, equally ancient, was that at least some diseases might be caused by invisible particles that could spread from one victim to another. "Just as there are seeds of things helpful to our life, so, for sure, others fly about that cause disease and death,"[2] the Roman poet Lucretius wrote in the first century B.C. In later centuries this idea was little regarded, however, because no one had any idea what these particles might be. To be sure, Antoni van Leeuwenhoek, a Dutch cloth seller whose hobby was making microscopes, reported in 1674 that his instruments revealed "little animals" in everything from rainwater to scrapings from his teeth. Relatively few people knew of his work, though, and neither he nor most other scientists associated the little animals with disease.

Researchers began to pay more attention to microorganisms (also called microbes or germs) after the 1860s, when French chemist-turned-microbiologist Louis Pasteur proved that these microscopic living things caused fermentation—the breakdown of plant material that produced beer and wine—and putrefaction—the decaying of meat, corpses, and other animal matter. Because disease often resembles putrefaction within a living body, Pasteur first theorized and, in the 1870s, accumulated evidence to prove that microbes caused at least some illnesses. Most scientists and physicians ridiculed this "germ theory" at first, but in the 1880s other brilliant researchers, such as German bacteriologist Robert Koch, confirmed and extended it by identifying the specific types of bacteria that caused tuberculosis, cholera, and a number of other infectious diseases.

The Birth of Magic Bullets

Even once this group of "enemies" was identified, physicians did not at first see drugs as the best way to fight them. As scientists such as Pasteur's protégé, Élie Metchnikoff, began to show in the 1880s, the body had its own soldiers, the cells and chemicals of the immune system. Most medical researchers of the late nineteenth century believed that the best way to prevent or cure disease was to make this system more effective. One way to do so was through vaccination, in which injection of small doses of weakened or killed disease microorganisms primed the immune system to recognize that type of microbe and destroy it quickly if it should ever enter the body again. Another way was to seek help from the immune systems of others. Animals such as horses were injected with disease-causing bacteria, and after their immune systems had reacted to the microbes, the serum, or liquid part of their blood, was harvested. This serum contained substances that could counteract the poisons made by the types of bacteria to which the animals had been exposed. "Serum therapy" was a successful treatment for such former killers as diphtheria and tetanus.

Paul Ehrlich, who did extensive research on the immune system before he became involved with developing drugs, also favored these immune-centered techniques at first. Indeed, he initially used the term *magic bullets* to refer to chemicals called antibodies, which the immune system creates as a means of marking microbes or other foreign substances for destruction by cells in the system. He called antibodies "magic" because each type attached itself to one specific kind of microorganism, causing the warrior cells to attack microbes only of that kind. All other microbes and body cells were left unharmed.

Ehrlich recognized, however, that the immune system's defenses did not always succeed, even with the help of vaccines and serums. In these cases, he thought, drugs might come to the rescue—if any could be found that, like antibodies, would destroy bacteria and other microorganisms without harming the body as well. Only drugs that could make this distinction would deserve to share the name of magic bullets, in Ehrlich's opinion. Although his systematic search for such compounds produced some valuable medicines, these drugs also caused severe side effects, so Ehrlich never felt that he had really succeeded in making a magic bullet.

Products of Nature's War

Ehrlich focused his search for magic bullets on dyes and other synthetic chemicals, but a few other researchers looked instead to products of the eternal competition among organisms that is mandated by evolution—a competition also often pictured as a war. Organisms' production of substances that kill or stop the growth of other organisms came to be known as antibiosis, and the compounds themselves were eventually called antibiotics.

French physician-researcher Paul Villemin coined the term *antibiosis* in 1889, but scientists had observed the phenomenon long before that. Louis Pasteur himself noted in 1877, for instance, that when animals infected with the bacteria that he and Robert Koch had shown to cause the deadly livestock disease anthrax were injected with soil microbes, they did not develop the disease as they normally would. Then, in the same year that Villemin began to speak of antibiosis, a German scientist named de Freudenreich ex-

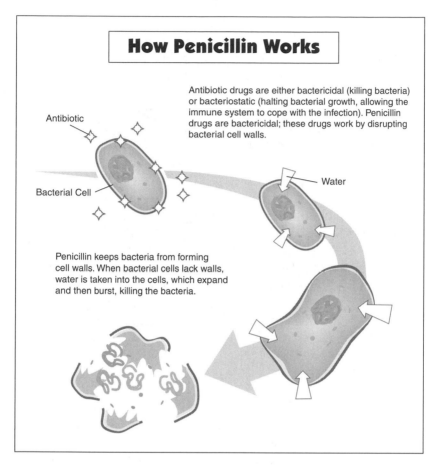

How Penicillin Works

Antibiotic drugs are either bactericidal (killing bacteria) or bacteriostatic (halting bacterial growth, allowing the immune system to cope with the infection). Penicillin drugs are bactericidal; these drugs work by disrupting bacterial cell walls.

Antibiotic

Bacterial Cell

Water

Penicillin keeps bacteria from forming cell walls. When bacterial cells lack walls, water is taken into the cells, which expand and then burst, killing the bacteria.

tracted a bluish substance from a type of bacteria that produced pus in wounds, and two other Germans, Rudolf Emmerich and Oskar Löw, found that this substance, which they called pyocyanase, destroyed a variety of dangerous bacteria in the test tube. Unfortunately, when they gave pyocyanase to patients, it proved both unstable and toxic. Although it was an antibacterial bullet of sorts (it continued to be used in wound ointments for several decades), pyocyanase clearly lacked the "magic" element required for Ehrlich's ideal drug.

By 1928, when a lucky laboratory accident introduced Scottish-born bacteriologist Alexander Fleming to the bacteria-killing properties of a substance made by the blue-green mold *Penicillium notatum*, most researchers had come to believe that magic bullets, either natural or synthetic, would never be found. This discouraging atmosphere was one of the reasons Fleming did not long pursue his research on this compound, which he called penicillin. The scientific mood changed, however, in the mid-1930s, after German researcher Gerhard Domagk, who, like Ehrlich, was seeking his bullets among dyes, discovered the first of what came to be known as the sulfa drugs. These drugs were not completely free of side effects, but they were relatively benign, and they stopped infection by several kinds of deadly microbes, including the ubiquitous streptococcus, which caused heart-damaging rheumatic fever as well as strep throat and wound infections.

The success of the sulfa drugs convinced researchers that magic bullets might be possible after all. In 1939, when Domagk was awarded the Nobel Prize in Physiology or Medicine for his discovery (though the Nazi government would not let him accept it), the editors of the highly respected British science journal *Nature* wrote that the sulfa drugs had produced "a revolutionary advance in therapeutics."[3] Although Australian-born Howard Florey's team at Britain's Oxford University was not at first looking for magic bullets when it began studying Fleming's penicillin at about this time, the existence of sulfa drugs probably influenced the direction of Florey's research.

Antibiotic Weapons

War—between humans this time—was also an influence. When Florey's group began testing penicillin on humans in 1940, Britain was already at war with Germany. War kept Britain from having the resources to develop the drug but, conversely, put its mass production on the pharmaceutical fast track in the United States after Florey brought his discovery there in 1941. American leaders saw penicillin as a potential key weapon in the battle against the country's human as well as bacterial enemies—as indeed it proved to be. "American penicillin won the war,"[4] states Rocko Fasanella, an emeritus ophthalmology professor at Yale University and amateur historian. Gilbert Shama, a microbiologist in the chemical engineering department of Loughborough University in Leicestershire, England, speculates that if the United States had not had penicillin to treat its soldiers or if Germany had also possessed the drug, Germany rather than the Allies might have won several crucial battles in the later part of World War II.

Given the circumstances of their birth, it was perhaps inevitable that the public went on viewing penicillin and the other antibiotics that soon followed it, such as streptomycin (1943), as war weapons even after the human conflict ended. As the press headlined the drugs' "miracle cures," physicians and patients alike came to see antibiotics (whose low toxicity to humans was as remarkable as their deadly effect on bacteria) as not merely the perfect embodiment of the magic bullets Ehrlich had dreamed of but as the microbiological equivalent of the atomic bomb. Fresh from the euphoria of victory over Germany and Japan, many Americans felt sure that an equally complete victory over disease-causing microbes would soon follow.

Bacterial "Enemies" Fight Back

A few scientists, including some of the pioneers of antibiotic development, thought otherwise. As early as 1942, French American researcher René Dubos, who had discovered gramicidin, the first modern antibiotic put into practical use in 1939 (like pyocyanase, it proved valuable for treating infections on the body's surface but was too toxic to take internally, so it never achieved the renown of penicillin and the others), warned that, sooner or later, bacteria were bound to develop resistance to antibiotics or, probably, any other drugs used against them. Alexander Fleming said the same thing in an interview published in the *New York Times* in 1945.

Among bacteria treated by an antibiotic, Dubos and Fleming explained, there were bound to be a few that happened to possess a way to disarm the drug. The antibiotic would kill or stop the growth of all the susceptible bacteria (many antibiotics do not kill bacteria directly; instead, they depend on the immune system to do that job after the antibiotic has stopped bacterial growth), but the resistant ones would remain and multiply rapidly. The danger of drug-resistant bacterial survivors was particularly great if low doses of antibiotics were used. Fleming noted:

> The greatest possibility of evil in self-medication [with penicillin] is the use of too small doses so that instead of clearing up infection, the microbes are educated to resist penicillin and a host of penicillin-fast [penicillin-resistant] organisms is bred out which can be passed to other individuals and from them to others until they reach someone who gets a septicemia or a pneumonia which penicillin cannot save.[5]

Resistance to the new "miracle drugs" was already occurring,

Fleming and Dubos pointed out. By the end of World War II, one survey reported that half the strains of the common wound-infecting bacterium *Staphylococcus aureus* that microbiologists checked were resistant to penicillin.

For the most part, these warnings fell on deaf ears. New antibiotics, and variations on old ones, were discovered or created so quickly during the late 1940s and early 1950s that most researchers believed that resistance would never become a serious problem. If resistance made old drugs useless, the reasoning went, new ones would replace them. If one antibiotic did not cure a particular infection, a different type or a combination of several types would surely do the job. Viewing humans and bacteria as engaged in an arms race much like the Cold War then taking place between the United States and the Soviet Union, the public and most scientists were positive that the humans would win. In 1969 Surgeon General William H. Stewart told Congress that science would soon "close the book on infectious diseases."[6]

The Antibiotic Paradox

In a war, armies usually do not wait for their enemies to attack. They strike first if they can, attempting to wipe out their foes before the opponents can gather full strength. If they are victorious, they sometimes show no mercy, killing everyone rather than taking prisoners. Armed with their new antibiotic arsenal, physicians fought disease in the same way. If doctors were unsure of the cause of a patient's illness, they often gave the person a broad-spectrum antibiotic (one that affects a wide variety of bacterial types) on the theory that it would be likely to slaughter the offending germs, whatever they might be. They did not worry about the fact that the antibiotic would also kill harmless bacteria in the patient's body, including those that might have protected health by competing with disease-causing microorganisms. Even when physicians suspected or knew that an illness was caused by viruses, which antibiotics do not affect, they sometimes prescribed an antibiotic anyway, just in case a secondary bacterial infection might start up.

Patients wanted to be equally sure of victory in the microbe war. Not understanding the difference between bacteria and viruses, many demanded antibiotics when they or their children suffered from virus-caused infections such as colds, flu, and middle ear inflammation—and physicians often complied rather than argued. In countries in which antibiotics were available without a prescription, which was the case in the United States until the mid-1950s and is true today in much of the developing world, people left physicians out of the equation entirely and simply dosed themselves. The "get them before they get you" mentality even led, in the 1990s, to the increasing use of household products containing

The production of penicillin and other antibiotics flourished after World War II, despite warnings that overuse could create drug-resistant bacteria.

antibacterial substances. Meanwhile, farmers and ranchers were giving millions of chickens, cattle, and other food animals low doses of antibiotics to prevent disease and promote rapid growth. As Alexander Fleming had pointed out in 1945, this kind of "subtherapeutic" use was ideal for creating resistant bacteria.

Far from guaranteeing the defeat of microorganisms, these and other misuses and overuses of antibiotics increased the evolutionary pressure on bacteria to develop the very resistance that would make the drugs useless. Stuart Levy of Boston's Tufts University calls this the antibiotic paradox. Indeed, as scientists came to understand more about bacterial genetics, they gained a new appreciation of bacteria's power to fight off humanity's supposedly invulnerable superweapons. The products of some genes inactivated the drugs; others protected the cellular targets that the antibiotics attacked, and still others pumped the compounds out of the bacterial cells before they could do harm. A bacterium resistant to one antibiotic usually proved resistant to all the drug's chemical cousins as well. Worst of all, researchers discovered that bacteria easily passed resistance genes from one species to another, even if the types were not closely related. This gene sharing meant that many bacteria soon became resistant to several different families of antibiotics. "The spread of genes is the problem, not just the spread of bacteria,"[7] writes microbiologist Abigail Salyers of the University of Illinois (Urbana-Champaign).

At the same time, a mixture of overconfidence and economics was reducing the flood of new antibiotics to a trickle. Stringent safety regulations in most Western countries today mean that developing and testing a new drug takes about a decade and is tremendously expensive. With infectious disease increasingly limited to the poor in such countries, pharmaceutical companies have had little incentive to invest effort and money in producing more antibiotics. Most of the antibiotics introduced from the 1960s onward have been variations on existing ones, which means that resistant microbes are already waiting for them when they first come out of the bottle.

Today, increasing numbers of common and deadly bacteria are immune to almost all of the 150 or so antibiotics that have been developed. Some researchers hope that persuading physicians and the public to use existing antibiotics more carefully and sparingly will slow the growth of resistance enough to allow more drugs to be created. They point to new types of antibiotics proposed or under development, including some made from natural compounds in the bodies of animals and humans and others designed on the basis of increased understanding of bacterial metabolism and genetics. Others suggest attacking bacteria with weapons other than antibiotics, such as bacteriophages (viruses that infect and destroy bacteria), vaccines, and probiotics ("good bacteria" that compete against disease-causing ones).

Pessimists, however, say that antibiotics and probably all other antimicrobial treatments are doomed. No matter what treatments are developed, they believe, bacteria will become resistant to them, and they will do so with increasing speed as different kinds of resistance genes accumulate and spread. The war against disease microbes will never end, or if it does, it will end in humanity's defeat. "Bacteria have outwitted us for ages, and will continue to do so,"[8] predicts Paula Fedorka-Cray, a scientist who works for the U.S. Department of Agriculture.

Need for a New Attitude

The only way to prevent a return to the dark ages of devastating epidemics in this "postantibiotic era," some of these experts feel, is to give up Western society's long-cherished belief in magic bullets and the warlike, oversimplistic "us or them" view of humans' relationship with microorganisms that underlies it. Microbes, they point out, do not have any intrinsic drive or desire to sicken or kill people. Many kinds, in fact, live harmlessly or even helpfully inside the human body. Microorganisms simply "want" what every other organism "wants"—to avoid damage, find enough food, and reproduce. Since disease-causing bacteria are parasites, living on or in other organisms (hosts), these last two goals usually require the ability to move from one host to another. By understanding microorganisms' needs and finding ways to fulfill them with minimal harm to humans, people can make microbial evolution work for them instead of against them. "Unless we play the evolutionary game consciously, we're going to be outwitted,"[9] says Harvard population biologist Richard Levins, a strong supporter of this new evolutionary view.

Paul Ewald, professor of global environmental studies (biology) at Amherst College in Massachusetts, agrees. He recommends discouraging methods of bacterial spread that do not require healthy hosts. One way to do this, he says, is to make sure that disease-causing bacteria are kept out of drinking water since bacterial transmission through water, unlike airborne transmission, does not require hosts who feel well enough to mingle with other people. Such actions would give microbes an evolutionary incentive to cause less serious illness, he believes.

Instead of seeing microorganisms as enemies to be destroyed, these experts say, people need to begin viewing them as neighbors with which humans must always coexist. If they can coexist peacefully, both may ultimately gain. As René Dubos wrote, "To regard any form of life merely as slave or foe will one day be considered poor philosophy, for all living things constitute an integral part of the cosmic order."[10]

Notes

1. Quoted in Ernst Bäumler, *Paul Ehrlich: Scientist for Life*. New York: Holmes and Meier, 1984, p. 108.

2. Quoted in Charles-Edward Amory Winslow, *The Conquest of Epidemic Disease: A Chapter in the History of Ideas*. Madison: University of Wisconsin Press, 1980, p. 82.

3. Quoted in *Current Biography Yearbook*, "Domagk, Gerhard (Johannes Paul)." New York: H.W. Wilson, 1958, p. 125.

4. Quoted in Edwin Kiester Jr., "A Curiosity Turned into the First Silver Bullet Against Death," *Smithsonian*, November 1990, p. 186.

5. Quoted in Stuart B. Levy, *The Antibiotic Paradox: How the Misuse of Antibiotics Destroys Their Curative Powers*. 2nd ed. Cambridge, MA: Perseus Books, 2002, p. 8.

6. Quoted in Elizabeth Pennisi, "U.S. Beefs Up CDC's Capabilities," *Science*, June 7, 1996, p. 1413.

7. Quoted in Christine Miot, "Antidotes for Antibiotic Use on the Farm," *BioScience*, November 2000, p. 956.

8. Quoted in Miot, "Antidotes for Antibiotic Use on the Farm," p. 957.

9. Quoted in Michael Shnayerson and Mark J. Plotkin, *The Killers Within: The Deadly Rise of Drug-Resistant Bacteria*. Boston: Little, Brown, 2003, p. 288.

10. Quoted in Carol L. Moberg, "René Dubos, a Harbinger of Microbial Resistance to Antibiotics," *Perspectives in Biology and Medicine*, Summer 1999, p. 559.

CHAPTER 1

Before Antibiotics

A Deadly Epidemic

By Giovanni Boccaccio

Giovanni Boccaccio (1313–1375), an Italian author who lived in Florence, lost many friends and family members in the epidemic called the Black Death (probably bubonic or pneumonic plague), which swept through Italy and much of the rest of Europe beginning in 1348. In the next several years he wrote a fictional work called *The Decameron*, containing a hundred stories that a group of Florentine lords and ladies who had fled to the countryside in the hope of escaping the epidemic supposedly told each other to pass the time.

The introduction to *The Decameron* describes the epidemic itself, including the massive social devastation it caused in Florence. According to Boccaccio, the disease came from Asia, but no one at the time knew exactly what caused it, let alone any way to cure it. Once symptoms appeared, he says, death almost always followed quickly. The feeling that they would soon die led many people to extreme behavior, he reports; some danced and drank constantly, while others embraced a monklike lifestyle. The illness was highly contagious, and fear of catching it led neighbors, friends, and even family members to abandon anyone who became sick. Many people died alone, he claims, and were buried in mass graves with a minimum of religious ritual. The epidemic affected rich and poor, country and city, making Florence a virtual city of the dead. Boccaccio's account provides a classic example of the destruction that diseases caused by bacteria could produce in the days before antibiotics were discovered.

Thirteen hundred and forty-eight years had passed since the fruitful Incarnation of the Son of God, when there came into the noble city of Florence, the most beautiful of all Italian cities, a deadly pestilence, which, either because of the operations

Giovanni Boccaccio, *The Decameron*, translated by M. Rigg. London: David Campbell, 1921.

of the heavenly bodies, or because of the just wrath of God mandating punishment for our iniquitous ways, several years earlier had originated in the Orient, where it destroyed countless lives, scarcely resting in one place before it moved to the next, and turning westward its strength grew monstrously. No human wisdom or foresight had any value: enormous amounts of refuse and manure were removed from the city by appointed officials, the sick were barred from entering the city, and many instructions were given to preserve health; just as useless were the humble supplications to God given not one time but many times in appointed processions, and all the other ways devout people called on God; despite all this, at the beginning of the spring of that year [1348], that horrible plague began with its dolorous effects in a most awe-inspiring manner, as I will tell you. And it did not behave as it did in the Orient, where if blood began to rush out the nose it was a manifest sign of inevitable death; but rather it began with swellings in the groin and armpit, in both men and women, some of which were as big as apples and some of which were shaped like eggs, some were small and others were large; the common people called these swellings gavaccioli. From these two parts of the body, the fatal gavaccioli would begin to spread and within a short while would appear over the entire body in various spots; the disease at this point began to take on the qualities of a deadly sickness, and the body would be covered with dark and livid [reddish] spots, which would appear in great numbers on the arms, the thighs, and other parts of the body; some were large and widely spaced while some were small and bunched together. And just like the gavaccioli earlier, these were certain indications of coming death.

Very Contagious

To cure these infirmities neither the advice of physicians nor the power of medicine appeared to have any value or profit; perhaps either the nature of the disease did not allow for any cure or the ignorance of the physicians (whose numbers, because men and women without any training in medicine invaded the profession, increased vastly) did not know how to cure it; as a consequence, very few were ever cured; all died three days after the appearance of the first outward signs, some lasted a little bit longer, some died a little bit more quickly, and some without fever or other symptoms. But what gave this pestilence particularly severe force was that whenever the diseased mixed with healthy people, like a fire through dry grass or oil it would rush upon the healthy. And this wasn't the worst of the evil: for not only did it infect healthy persons who conversed or mixed with the sick, but also touching bread or any other object which had been handled or worn by the sick would transport the sickness from the victim to the one touching the object. It is a wondrous tale that I have to tell: if I were not one of many people who saw it with their own eyes, I would scarcely have dared to believe it, let alone to write it down, even if I had heard it from a completely trustworthy person. I say that the pestilence I have been describing was so contagious, that not only did it visibly pass from one person to another, but also, whenever an animal other than a human being touched anything belonging to a person who had died from the disease, I say not only did it become contaminated by the sickness, but also died literally within the instant. Of all these things, as I have said before, my own eyes had experience many times: once, the rags of a poor man who had just died from the disease were thrown into the public street and were noticed by two pigs, who, following their custom, pressed their snouts into the rags, and afterwards picked them up with their teeth, and shook them against their cheeks: and within a short time, they both began to convulse, and they both, the two of them, fell dead on the ground next to the evil rags.

Strange Behavior

Because of all these things, and many others that were similar or even worse, diverse fears and imaginings were born in those left alive, and all of them took recourse to the most cruel precaution: to avoid and run away from the sick and their things; by doing this, each person believed they could preserve their health. Others were of the opinion that they should live moderately and guard against all excess; by this means they would avoid infection. Having withdrawn, living separate from everybody else, they settled down and locked themselves in, where no sick person or any other living person could come, they ate small amounts of food and drank the most delicate wines and avoided all luxury, refraining from speech with outsiders, refusing news of the dead or the sick or anything else, and diverting themselves with music or whatever else was pleasant. Others, who disagreed with this, affirmed that drinking beer, enjoying oneself, and going around singing and ruckus-raising and satisfying all one's appetites whenever possible and laughing at the whole bloody thing was the best medicine; and these people put into practice what they heartily advised to others: day and night, going from tavern to tavern, drinking without moderation or measure, and many times going from house to house drinking up a storm and only listening to and talking about pleasing things. These parties were easy to find because everyone behaved as if they were going to die soon, so they cared nothing about themselves nor their belongings; as a result, most houses became common property, and any stranger passing by could enter and use the house as if he were its master. But for all their bestial living, these people always ran away from the sick. With so much affliction and misery, all reverence for the laws, both of God and of man, fell apart and dissolved, because the ministers and executors of the laws were either dead or ill like everyone else, or were left with so few officials that they were unable to do their duties; as a result, everyone was free to do whatever they pleased. Many other people steered a middle course between these two extremes, neither restricting their diet like the first group, nor indulging so liberally in drinking and other forms of dissolution like the second group, but simply not going beyond their needs or satisfying their appetite beyond the necessary, and, instead of locking themselves away, these people walked about freely, holding in their hands a posy [bouquet] of flowers, or fragrant herbs, or diverse exotic spices, which sometimes they pressed to their nostrils, believing it would comfort the brain with smells of that sort because the stink of corpses, sick bodies, and medicines polluted the air all about the city. Others held a more cruel opinion, one that in the end probably guaranteed their safety, saying that there was no better or more effective medicine against the disease than to run away from it; convinced by this argument, and caring for no-one but themselves, huge numbers of men and women abandoned their rightful city, their rightful homes, their relatives and their parents and their things, and sought out the countryside, as if the wrath of God would punish the iniquities of men with this plague based on where they happened to be, as if the wrath of God was aroused against only those who unfortunately found themselves within the city walls, or as if the whole of the population of the city would be exterminated in its final hour.

Of all these people with these various opinions, not all died, nor did they all survive; on the contrary, many from each camp fell ill in all places, and having, when they were healthy, set an example to all those who remained healthy, they languished in their illness completely alone, having been abandoned by everybody. One citizen avoided another, everybody neglected their neighbors and rarely or never visited their parents and relatives unless from a distance; the ordeal had so withered the hearts of men and women that brother abandoned brother, and the uncle abandoned his nephew and the sister her brother and many times, wives abandoned their husbands, and, what is even more incredible and cruel, mothers and fathers abandoned their children and would refuse to visit them. As a result, of that innumerable number of those, men and women, who fell ill, there remained no-one to care for them except for friends, which were very few, or avaricious servants, who, despite the high salaries and easy service, became very scarce. And there were some men and women of such vulgar mind, that most of them were not accustomed to service, and did nothing other than serve things whenever the sick person asked and watch while they died; and the wages of this service was often death. And some of the sick were totally abandoned by neighbors, relatives, and friends, and, on account of the scarcity of servants, turned to a custom no-one had ever heard of before: no sick woman, even if she were a svelte, beautiful, and gentle lady, would care if she were being served by a man, young or otherwise, and would have no shame exposing every part of her body to him as if he were another woman, if the necessity of her sickness required her to; and this is why the women who were cured were a little less chaste afterwards. Moreover, many people died by chance who would have survived had they been helped. And so, because of the shortage of people to care for the sick, and the violence of the disease, day and night such a multitude died that it would dumbfound any to hear of it who did not see it themselves. As a result, partly out of necessity, there arose customs among those surviving that were contrary to the original customs of the city.

Customs Change

There used to be a custom, which is today still followed, where the women relatives and neighbors of a dead person would gather in the house and there mourn; on the other hand, there would gather at the front of the dead man's house neighbors and other citizens as well, whose numbers followed from the quality of the deceased man, and along with these priests in their finery, and with all the funeral pomp and candles and singing, he would be carried by those closest to him to the church of his choice. When the ferocity of the pestilence began to mount, for the most part people ceased with this custom and replaced it with a far different one. For not only did many people die without women surrounding them, most passed away from this life without anyone there to witness it at all; there were very few who departed amid the pious wailing and beloved tears of those close to them, far from this, most took up the custom of laughing and partying while their loved ones died; this latter usage, the women, who formerly had been so merciful and concerned with the health of the deceased one's soul, especially mastered. Also, it became rare for the body to be born to the church accompanied by more than ten or twelve men, who were not noble and cherished citizens, but a kind of grave-digger fraternity made up of the least men of the city (they demanded to be called sextons [church employees], and demanded high wages) who would bear them away; and these would bear the body quickly away, not to the church the dead man had asked for, but to the nearest one they could find, with four to six priests, maybe with a candle but sometimes not, in front; and with the help of these sextons, without fatiguing themselves with any long ceremony or rite, in any old tomb that they found unoccupied they'd dump the corpse.

Corpses Pile Up

As for the lesser people, who were for the most part middle class, they presented the most miserable spectacle: for these, who had no hope or who were seized with poverty, had to remain in the area, and fell ill by the thousands every day, and since they had no servants or any other kind of help, almost without exception all of them died. And many would meet their end in the public streets both day and night, and many others, who met their ends in their own houses, would first come to the attention of their neighbors because of the stench of their rotting corpses more than anything else; and with these and others all dying, there were corpses everywhere. And the neighbors always followed a particular routine, more out of fear of being corrupted by the corpse than out of charity for the deceased. These, either by themselves or with the help of others when available, would carry the corpse of the recently deceased from the house and leave it lying in the street outside where, especially in the morning, a countless number of corpses could be seen lying about. Funeral biers would come, and if there was a shortage of funeral biers, some other flat table or something or other would be used to place the corpses on. Nor did it infrequently happen that a single funeral bier would carry two or three people at the same time, but rather one frequently saw on a single bier a husband and a wife, two or three brothers, a father and a son, or some other relatives. And an infinite number of times it happened that two priests bearing a cross would be going to bury someone when three or four other biers, being born by bearers, would follow behind them; the priests would believe themselves to be heading for a single burial, and would find, when they arrived at the churchyard, that they had six or eight more burials following behind them. Nor were there ever tears or candles or any company honoring the dead; things had reached such a point, that people cared no more for the death of other people than they did for the death of a goat: for this thing, death, which even the wise never accept with patience, even though it occur rarely and relatively unobtrusively, had appeared manifestly to even the smallest intellects, but the catastrophe was so unimaginably great that nobody really cared. There was such a multitude of corpses that arrived at all churches every day and every hour, that sacred burial ground ran out, which was especially a problem if each person wanted their own plot in accordance with ancient custom. When the cemeteries were for the most part full, they excavated great pits in which they'd place hundreds of newly arrived corpses, and each corpse would be covered with a thin layer of dirt until the pit was filled.

Pervading the Country and the City

And beyond all the particulars we suffered in the city, I will tell you not only about the ill times passing through the city, but also mention that the countryside was not spared these circumstances. For here, in the fortified towns, similar things occurred but on a lesser scale than in the city, through the small villages and through the camps of the miserable and poor laborers and their families, without any care from physicians or help from servants, and in the highways and the fields and their houses, day and night at whatever hour, not like humans but more like animals they died; and because of this, they came to neglect their customs, as did the people in the city, and had no concern for their belongings. Beyond all this, they began to behave as if every day were the day of their certain death, and they did no work to provide for their future needs by caring for their fields or their animals, but rather consumed everything they owned. Because of this, it happened that oxen, asses, sheep, goats, pigs, chickens, and dogs, the most faithful human companions, were driven from the houses, and in the fields, where the crops had been abandoned, not even reaped let alone gathered, they would wander about at their pleasure; and many, as if they possessed human reason, after they had pastured all day long, would return satiated to their houses without any guidance from any shepherd.

Let us leave the countryside and return to the city; how much more can be said of the cruelty of heaven, and possibly, in part, that of humanity, which between March and July of that year, because of the ferocity of the pestilence and the fact that many of the sick were poorly cared for or abandoned in their hour of need by people frightened for their health, killed off one hundred thousand human creatures for certain within the walls of the city of Florence. Who, before this fatal calamity, would have thought there were so many within the city? Oh, how many grand palaces, how many beautiful homes, how many noble dwellings, filled with families, with lords and ladies, became completely emptied even of children! Oh, how many famous families, how many vast estates, how many renowned fortunes remained without any rightful successors! How many noble men, how many beautiful ladies, how many light-hearted youth, who were such that Galen, Hippocrates, or Asclepius [famous physicians of the ancient world] would declare them the healthiest of all humans, had breakfast in the morning with their relatives, companions, or friends, and had dinner that evening in another world with their ancestors!

Microorganisms Cause Disease

By Patrice Debré

Famous nineteenth-century French scientist Louis Pasteur was trained as a chemist, but early in his career he began studying bacteria and other microorganisms, about which almost nothing was known at the time. He eventually became convinced that these microscopic creatures caused many illnesses that could be spread from one person or animal to another. Few other scientists, however, believed him. This selection from a biography of Pasteur by Patrice Debré, head of the biological immunology laboratory at the Pitié-Salpétrière Hospital in Paris, describes how Pasteur showed that bacteria caused anthrax, a deadly and widespread disease that chiefly affected cattle and sheep.

Pasteur began investigating anthrax in 1877 at the request of France's minister of agriculture, Debré reports, because the disease was producing great economic losses for French farmers. Scientists had found rod-shaped microorganisms in the blood of animals with anthrax beginning in the early 1850s, he says, but it was by no means clear that these microorganisms caused the disease. For instance, animals injected with blood from other animals that had died of anthrax almost always died quickly, but sometimes no rod-shaped microbes could be found in the second group's blood. According to Debré, Pasteur performed experiments that explained these puzzling results. Pasteur demonstrated that the rod-shaped germs caused anthrax but that some of the animals that had died after receiving blood from anthrax-containing corpses had been killed by a second kind of bacterium that appeared in the blood after death. Pasteur's work on anthrax provided convincing proof of the germ (microorganism) theory of disease. Knowing that bacteria could cause disease led scientists to look for ways to stop them, a line of research that eventually led to the discovery of antibiotics.

Pasteur's work on the origin of infectious diseases now took a detour through veterinary medicine. In early 1877, he began by looking into anthrax at the request of the Minister of Agriculture, who had been alerted by the departmental council of Eure-et-Loir [a district in France]. Pasteur, who had not long before triumphed over the scourges [diseases] of the silkworm, would no doubt be able to find a remedy against an ill that was devastating the flocks [of sheep and cattle].

A Deadly Livestock Disease

Anthrax was one of the most murderous diseases for domestic animals. It existed in many parts of the world, including Russia, where it was called "Siberian plague." Most French departments [districts], particularly in the central regions, suffered its ruinous effects. Horses, oxen, cows, and sheep were attacked in varying degrees. Victims were counted in the hundreds of thousands.

The situation was particularly bad in the department of Eure-et-Loir. Not one farm escaped the disease and the farmers considered themselves lucky if losses amounted to no more than 5 percent of their livestock. Since the calamity struck without warning, they blamed it on supposedly poisoned pastures, and there was talk of anthrax farms and cursed meadows. The sick animals had fallen under an evil spell, and the rare ones that survived had been saved by a miracle. Occasionally, humans could also be affected: shepherds, butchers, knackers [buyers of old or sick animals to slaughter and make pet food], or tanners [people who made leather from animal skins] were in grave danger from a simple scratch, a small cut when they came in contact with a dead or dying animal.

Where did this ill come from? How was it spread? All the names by which it was called in the eighteenth and nineteenth centuries (evil fire, the black illness, gangrene, anthrax) and the picturesque descriptions that went with them betray the ignorance and the helplessness of the rural practitioners. Since the dead bodies seemed to be burnt or charred, external causes were incriminated, such as the action of the sun, perspiration, summer heat waves. Also accused were stagnant water, the irritating bites of flies and horse-flies, spoiled fodder [animal feed] crawling with insects. Marshes were suspected, particularly in the [region of] Sologne. The most generally accepted hypothesis postulated a poisoning by toxic herbs that corrupted the humors [body fluids].

The disease would strike in a few hours. Falling behind in the flock, the sick animal, its head lowered, breathing heavily and quivering, soon fell down on the grass, soiling it with bloody dejecta [excrement]. Blood flowed from the mouth and the nostrils. Without a sound, the animal collapsed and often died so quickly that all the hapless shepherd could do was to pronounce it dead. Lying on its back with its legs up in the air, or leaning against a partition in the stable, the sheep presented a huge distended belly. If a knife was thrust into the still warm cadaver, thick, viscous, and blackish blood would ooze out, a kind of ink-colored mush. If an autopsy was performed, it revealed an enormous spleen [an organ in the abdomen that makes blood cells]—hence another name sometimes given to the disease by way of a descriptive foreshortening of a symbolic but also explanatory nature: "spleen blood disease."

The first veterinarians who encountered this disease showed that it could be transmitted, but they did not push their reasoning to the point of speaking of a contagious disease pure and simple. In experiments inspired by those of [the famous French physiologist of the early nineteenth-century François] Magendic, they injected healthy animals with putrefied matter and interpreted the results as poisoning rather than contagion. This erroneous judgment is understandable, considering that poison was known from time immemorial, whereas the murderous effects of bacteria had barely begun to be demonstrated. At Chartres, the capital of the disease, rumor therefore accused a mysterious poison, a telluric miasma [a gas rising from the earth] that was supposed to intensify during the heat of summer, of killing the animal as it blackened its blood and caused its spleen to bulge.

Mysterious Microbes

In the early 1850s, Davaine, who, as [Emile] Duclaux put it so strikingly, "looked at medicine through the windows of science," was one of the first to notice little rod-shaped microorganisms in anthrax-blood. Casimir-Joseph Davaine, born in 1812, was a physician. A native of Saint-Amand-les-Eaux in the department of Nord, he and his colleague [Pierre François Olive] Rayer had carried out an extensive investigation of anthrax in cattle. Their studies, which followed those of [Onesime] Delafond, a veterinarian at the veterinary school of Alfort, and of [Franz] Pollender and [Friedrich] Brauell in Germany, had the merit of drawing attention to microscopic organisms that could be observed in the blood of the dying animals. But this was precisely why they were contested and debated. Davaine had understood that the organisms were not normal constituent parts of the blood, corpuscles or webs of fibrin serum, but foreign particles, which he classified as plants. This insight would not have distinguished Davaine from other illustrious explorers of endemic disease if he had not at the same time asked the essential question: was this a contagious agent or simply a tangible but inoffensive consequence of the disease?

It took nearly thirty years to answer this question. Although it had been stated correctly enough, it did have the unfortunate effect of jumbling the tracks it had exposed. To begin with, since the corpuscle detected in the anthrax blood was assumed to be of plant origin, a few obstinate observers proposed to go so far as to consider it a seed or a spore. This was indeed a perspicacious idea, considering that it was later discovered that a bacterium can sporulate [form spores] by changing its form. But since the specific anthrax bacillus is small, it was confused with the usual germs of putrefaction and therefore went unnoticed for a long time. Davaine was the first to isolate it, but he did not fully realize the implications of his observation: in a notice about his own work he published shortly thereafter, he did not even mention this discovery—and it was to take him twelve years to recognize its importance.

It was only in 1861, when he became aware of Pasteur's work on fermentation, that Davaine made the connection with what he himself had written earlier. He was struck above all by the description of the butyric ferment [a type of bacteria], whose cylindrical rod shape resembled that of the corpuscles in the anthrax blood. In 1863, Davaine therefore took another look at his observation of 1850 and gave another paper to the Academy of Sciences on the lethal role of the anthrax bacillus. In his note he explicitly acknowledged Pasteur's work.

Conflicting Conclusions

As Pasteur pointed out, 1863 was the year in which the experiments carried out in the laboratory of the rue d'Ulm [Pasteur's Paris laboratory] were demonstrating that blood and urine gathered under aseptic conditions remained sterile, proving that there were no pre-existing germs in the internal environment. Spontaneous generation, in other words, did not occur in the human body any more than in swan-necked flasks.

During that same year a physician in Dourdain, the neighbor of a farmer who in one week lost twelve sheep to anthrax, sent Davaine a sample of the blood taken from one of the cadavers. Examination under the microscope once again revealed the immobile and transparent bacteria that were assumed to be specific to anthrax. When he inoculated rabbits with this blood, Davaine saw them die in short order.

One might think that the demonstration was made: here was the bacterium, and here was death; the connection seemed straightforward. But then the blood could also contain other elements than bacteria, and so it was not difficult to contest the hypothesis. Before long, Davaine's theory was indeed contradicted by two professors at Val-de-Grâce, Pierre-François Jaillard and Emile Leplat, who repeated the experiment, using cow's blood that they had shipped in the middle of summer from a knacker's yard. Their finding was quite different: although the rabbits did die from the inoculation of the cursed blood, not a single bacterium was found in their cadavers. The conclusion was obvious: the bacterium was an epiphenomenon [something associated with but not really related to a disease]. Davaine in turn repeated Jaillard and Leplat's experiments and confirmed their observation, but he proposed a new interpretation: since they had used a cow and not a sheep, Jaillard and Leplat were dealing with a new disease different from anthrax. Under these circumstances, why not call it a cow disease. This, however, was as far as Davaine was able to go.

Robert Koch's Experiments

Some fifteen years later, Koch's experiments became known. Born near Hanover [Germany] in 1843, Robert Koch was thirty-three years old when he became interested in this problem. At the time he was practicing in Wollstein in the province of Posnan after studying in Göttingen and Berlin, where he had come in contact with the most eminent scientists of the day, among them Jacob Henle. The latter had given him an understanding of the microbe theory [of disease] and the theoretical and experimental obstacles it was facing. Koch was to reap glory and immortality when he discovered the tuberculosis bacillus in 1882 and the cholera vibrio in 1883, but for the moment he spent his time at the bedside of sick farmers, an occupation that also gave him the opportunity to observe anthrax in flocks of farm animals. In a primitive laboratory he had set up in his home, he tackled this problem by himself, seeking to repeat and supersede Davaine's observations.

In doing so, he first sought to find a culture medium for the anthrax bacteria. It occurred to him to use some drops of the aqueous humor from the eye of an ox or a rabbit. This medium seemed particularly suitable for nourishing the germ, for within a few hours he observed that the rods were becoming longer, forming a kind of tangle of threads that filled the visual field of the microscope. Examining the entire length of the corpuscles, Koch noticed ovoid elements arranged like peas in a pod; these he placed into the category of spores. This observation was close to the descriptions Pasteur had published in his studies of the flacherie [a disease] of the silkworm. It was thus established that bacteria can sporulate and come back to life from these spores several years later. In his search for the anthrax bacillus, Koch was thus no longer guided by Pasteur's work in the chemistry of fermentation but by his research on the silkworm moth.

When Koch placed a few pieces of spleen taken from diseased animals into the aqueous humor of the eyes, the inoculation with the rods, like that with the spores, produced as severe a disease as when it was transmitted by blood from the spleen. Thus it was possible to reproduce in a living medium what had been observed under the microscope. For the second time, a scientist had come close to the goal, and the problem seemed almost totally solved: the black disease was caused by the *bacillus anthracis.*

At this point, the French physiologist Paul Bert provided new arguments to the opposition, and thereby led Pasteur to join the fray. In January 1877, Bert announced to the Biological Society that it was possible to kill the *bacillus anthracis* in a drop of blood by means of compressed oxygen; yet if one inoculated the remainder of the blood, disease and death would ensue even though no bacterium could be seen. "Bacteridia are therefore neither the cause nor the necessary effect of anthrax disease," he concluded.

Proving a Theory

It now fell to Pasteur to lift the last doubts and perfect an argumentation that had not been entirely convincing. For his experiments he obtained the assistance of one of his former students at the Ecole normale [a college for training teachers], Jules Joubert, now professor at the Collège Rollin (today Lycée Jacques-Decour) in Paris. The first problem to be solved was to demonstrate beyond any doubt the role of the bacterium, and then to eliminate any deleterious [damaging] influence that could be attributed to the blood, to the serum, or even to other microorganisms.

Ever since his studies on beer, Pasteur had surrounded himself by an arsenal of culturing techniques. On the shelves in his laboratory he could find test tubes and media that allowed him to make bacteria proliferate whenever he needed them. He also knew that a germ, even if highly diluted, can multiply sufficiently to invade

Louis Pasteur's work on the origin of infectious diseases eventually led scientists to the discovery of antibiotics.

the preparation if given a favorable environment. It was this property that Pasteur set out to exploit first. The experiment was simple: in order to demonstrate that the bacterium alone transmits the disease, all he had to do was to dilute a drop of anthrax blood and at the same time create conditions favoring microbial proliferation. Through a veterinarian in Chartres, Boutet, Pasteur obtained a sample of the blood of an animal that had recently died of anthrax. One drop taken from this bacterial focus was diluted in urine, a medium that favored its development. After a period of culturing sufficient to permit the germs to reproduce and the blood to become diluted, Pasteur took another drop from this solution and placed it into a second flask of fresh urine, where the incubation was repeated. Then another drop was taken and also diluted, and this process was continued until, at the end of some ten passages and culturings, "the original drop of blood, the one that furnished the first seed, has been drowned in an ocean as it were."

"Only the bacterium," added Duclaux, "has escaped dilution, for it multiplies in each one of the cultures." The culturing was indeed so effective and so rapid that within a few hours the liquid took on a whitish and matted look, as if a wad of carded [combed] cotton had been dissolved in it. All that remained was to inject a rabbit with one drop of the product of the last passage. The result was beyond contradiction: this inoculation killed as surely as if anthrax blood had been used. Pasteur had thus performed a conclusive experiment to show that the disease was indeed transmitted by the bacterium. The virulence could be inherent neither in the sticky red blood corpuscles or other constituent parts of the blood, for these were too diluted to interfere, nor in some filterable virus, for if the preparation was filtered, it was no longer lethal. For Pasteur, the matter was perfectly clear: anthrax was indeed a disease caused by a specific bacterium, just as scabies [a skin disease] is caused by a mite—the only difference being that in order to see the germ one needs a microscope with its enlarging lenses.

Solving Mysteries

Meanwhile, he still had to explain the experiments of Jaillard and Leplat, as well as Paul Bert's enigma. How could the former have injected guinea pigs with anthrax blood without subsequently finding a trace of the bacillus in the animals, which nonetheless were almost immediately killed by the injection? And why did the latter, having used a procedure that eliminated all visible traces of the germ, continue to see its virulence intact?

More inventive than Davaine, Pasteur refused to go along with the preconceived notion that everything that is happening in the rest of the body also happens in the blood. More imaginative as well, he put forth the hypothesis of a second disease. To begin with, he decided to reproduce the conditions of the experiments supporting Davaine's opponents, namely summer heat and the delayed shipping of the cadavers, in a word, conditions that favored putrefaction. From his earlier research, Pasteur remembered in particular that the decomposition of organic matter is due to specific germs. That is why, accompanied again by the veterinarian Boutet, he went to a knacker's yard near Chartres so that he could personally supervise the taking of anthrax blood. He carefully chose three cadavers whose state of preservation exactly reproduced the experiments of Leplat and Jaillard.

On 13 June 1877, in this knacker's yard near Chartres, Pasteur had before him three cadavers, one sheep that had died sixteen hours earlier, a horse whose death had occurred twenty-four hours before, and a cow that must have been dead for at least two days, since it had been brought from a fairly remote place. Three animal corpses, three time frames, three results from the analysis: the blood of the recently deceased sheep contained many anthrax bacilli; the blood of the horse contained very few, and that of the cow, none at all.

Ever since his groping attempts to understand the silkworm problem, Pasteur knew that two diseases can crisscross and interfere with one another. If this was the case here, he had to produce evidence for a second agent of infection that could not be seen in the blood. As was only logical, Pasteur turned to the blood of the cow, where the anthrax bacillus could not be detected, to find that second agent. He injected a sample of it into the belly of a guinea pig and observed. Within a few hours, the animal presented a distended abdomen and swollen muscles. At the autopsy, Pasteur recorded pockets of gas and a running serosity [oozing of fluid] in the abdomen. Having very carefully removed some of this brackish [foul] liquid and examined it under the microscope, Pasteur found in it a set of new microbes, germs of putrefaction. Everything became clear. There was indeed a second disease, this one related to the microbes of putrefaction, anaerobic germs that were paralyzed by air and could be easily observed only in the body of the injected guinea pig.

Two Diseases

How could this phenomenon have remained unknown for so long, Pasteur asked himself. Simply because the experimenters were in the habit of examining the blood of cadavers without thinking of looking for the germ elsewhere. "Yet the fact is, not only that the microbes examined here appear last in the blood, but also that in this liquid one of them takes on a very special appearance, a great length that often exceeds the total diameter of the field of vision of the microscope and such translucency that it can easily elude observation. . . . If one takes the trouble to look for it elsewhere, one finds in the tissues and in the serosity of a putrefying animal great masses of these proliferating germs." The second disease was related, then, to a new germ to which Pasteur gave the name "septic vibrio," a term that was to become famous in every language.

In this manner Davaine's theory and the counter-experiments of Leplat and Jaillard were reconciled, for although the septic vibrio was not present in the blood of the sheep that had died most recently, it appeared later in the blood of the animal whose cadaver had for some time lain abandoned on a manure heap.

As for Paul Bert's enigma, it too was solved by Pasteur's discovery. It turned out that the germ whose involvement he had demonstrated was anaerobic. So what had Paul Bert done when he subjected anthrax blood to a stream of oxygen under high pressure? He had, to be sure, suppressed the rapid movements of the septic vibrio through contact with the air, "but this does not mean that the vibrio was killed, for the contact with oxygen transforms it into corpuscles/germs, so that overnight a liquid filled with organized and motile filaments will be reduced to a jumble of extremely weak luminous specks. But if these specks are introduced into the body of a guinea pig or into an appropriate liquid, they reproduce as motile filiform [moving, threadlike] vibrios and the animal dies with all the expected symptoms."

Disease from Decay

As for characterizing the vibrio and the disease it produces, Pasteur took his clue from an observation made by a Parisian veterinarian, Signol. In December 1875, Signol had sent to the Academy of Sciences a note in which he showed that the blood of healthy animals killed by a blow or asphyxiation, if drawn from the deep veins connected to the intestine, becomes virulent after a few hours. If inoculated, this blood causes a death similar to the kind from anthrax. Commissioned to verify this finding, Pasteur repeated the experiment in January 1876 and found the same phenomenon. But he also detected an additional fact: among the microbes of putrefaction, he noticed a germ that "pushed the blood corpuscles aside in its undulant and creeping movement." At the time, the significance of this observation eluded him, but later, when he was engaged in the search for the origin of the septic vibrio, Pasteur remembered this earlier observation. Now, with that synthetic insight that so often led to his most important conclusions, he stated that the second disease described was the one that is transmitted by putrefied cadavers that are left to rot in the summer heat. Consequently, the septic vibrio "is none other than one of the vibrios of putrefaction. . . . Its germ must exist almost everywhere, and surely also in the matter contained in the intestinal tract. When a cadaver is discarded and if it still contains its intestine, the latter promptly becomes the focus of a putrefaction. At this point, the septic vibrio is bound to spread throughout the serosity, the humors, and the blood of the internal organs of the cadaver."

Germs Cause Disease

These discoveries concerning the anthrax bacterium and the septic vibrio thus definitively established the microbe theory of disease. By virtue of their ingeniousness and their precision, Pasteur's experimental techniques had triumphed and shed light on areas where others had gotten lost in an overly sophisticated chiaroscuro. It had now been established once and for all that two different kinds of infection could be caused by two different germs, with one of them, the septic vibrio, developing in case of putrefaction. Beyond these two specific instances, Pasteur also showed that he was able to identify the agents of contagion and describe in every detail the diseases for which they are responsible. Yet, despite the absolute clarity of the demonstration, it was to take years of effort to win over certain minds blinded by prejudice and make them acknowledge that here was the point of departure for a general theory of infectious disease.

Killing Germs in Wounds

By Joseph Lister

In the 1860s, even before Louis Pasteur had announced his belief that microorganisms could cause disease, English surgeon Joseph Lister read accounts of experiments in which Pasteur had shown that microorganisms could live in the air and could cause putrefaction (decay) in animal matter such as meat. Noticing a similarity between putrefaction and the wound infections that often killed people in his hospital wards, Lister deduced that germs might cause these infections as well. He concluded that if he could kill germs in wounds, he might prevent the infections.

In the following article from the *British Medical Journal* of 1867, Lister reports that he has successfully used a chemical called carbolic acid to clean wounds. He describes applying it to wound dressings in several cases of compound fracture, in which a broken bone penetrates the skin and produces an open wound. He explains how dressings with carbolic acid paste can protect even large wounds, saving limbs that normally would have to be amputated. He also shows how the treatment can be applied to abscesses, another type of infected wound. He points out that his treatment has essentially eliminated wound infections from his surgical ward at the Glasgow (Scotland) Royal Infirmary, saving many lives. Until antibiotics were developed, variations on Lister's antiseptic treatment, which killed germs on the body's surface but could not be applied inside the body, were practically the only way to prevent infection.

I n the course of an extended investigation into the nature of inflammation, and the healthy and morbid conditions of the blood in relation to it, I arrived several years ago at the conclusion that the essential cause of suppuration in wounds is de-

Joseph Lister, "On the Antiseptic Principle of the Practice of Surgery," *British Medical Journal*, September 21, 1867.

composition, brought about by the influence of the atmosphere upon blood or serum retained within them, and, in the case of contused wounds, upon portions of tissue destroyed by the violence of the injury.

A Germ-Killing Chemical

To prevent the occurrence of suppuration with all its attendant risks was an object manifestly desirable, but till lately apparently unattainable, since it seemed hopeless to attempt to exclude the oxygen which was universally regarded as the agent by which putrefaction was effected. But when it had been shown by the researches of Pasteur that the septic properties of the atmosphere depended not on the oxygen, or any gaseous constituent, but on minute organisms suspended in it, which owed their energy to their vitality, it occurred to me that decomposition in the injured part might be avoided without excluding the air, by applying as a dressing some material capable of destroying the life of the floating particles. Upon this principle I have based a practice of which I will now attempt to give a short account.

The material which I have employed is carbolic or phenic acid, a volatile organic compound, which appears to exercise a peculiarly destructive influence upon low forms of life, and hence is the most powerful antiseptic with which we are at present acquainted.

Compound Fractures

The first class of cases to which I applied it was that of compound fractures, in which the effects of decomposition in the injured part were especially striking and pernicious. The results have been such as to establish conclusively the great principle that all local inflammatory mischief and general febrile disturbances which follow severe injuries are due to the irritating and poisonous influence of decomposing blood or sloughs. For these evils are entirely avoided by the antiseptic treatment, so that limbs which would otherwise be unhesitatingly condemned to amputation may be retained, with confidence of the best results.

In conducting the treatment, the first object must be the destruction of any septic germs which may have been introduced into the wounds, either at the moment of the accident or during the time which has since elapsed. This is done by introducing the acid of full strength into all accessible recesses of the wound by means of a piece of rag held in dressing forceps and dipped into the liquid. This I did not venture to do in the earlier cases; but experience has shown that the compound which carbolic acid forms with the blood, and also any portions of tissue killed by its caustic action, including every parts of the bone, are disposed of by absorption and organisation, provided they are afterwards kept from decomposing. We are thus enabled to employ the antiseptic treatment efficiently at a period after the occurrence of the injury at which it would otherwise probably fail. Thus I have now under my care, in Glasgow Infirmary, a boy who was admitted with compound fracture of the leg as late as eight and one-half hours after the accident, in whom, nevertheless all local and constitutional [whole body] disturbance was avoided by means of carbolic acid, and the bones were soundly united five weeks after his admission.

Protecting Large Wounds

The next object to be kept in view is to guard effectually against the spreading of decomposition into the wound along the stream of blood and serum which oozes out during the first few days after the accident, when the acid originally applied has been washed out or dissipated by absorption and evaporation. This part of the treatment has been greatly improved during the past few weeks. The method which I have hitherto published (see *Lancet* for Mar. 16th, 23rd, 30th, and April 27th, 1867) consisted in the application of a piece of lint dipped in the acid, overlapping the sound skin to some extent and covered with a tin cap, which was daily raised in order to touch the surface of the lint with the antiseptic. This method certainly succeeded well with wounds of moderate size; and indeed I may say that in all the many cases of this kind which have been so treated by myself or my house-surgeons, not a single failure has occurred. When, however, the wound is very large, the flow of blood and serum is so profuse, especially during the first twenty-four hours, that the antiseptic application cannot prevent the spread of decomposition into the interior unless it overlaps the sound skin for a very considerable distance, and this was inadmissible by the method described above, on account of the extensive sloughing of the surface of the cutis [skin] which it would involve. This difficulty has, however, been overcome by employing, a paste composed of common whiting (carbonate of lime), mixed with a solution of one part of carbolic acid in four parts of boiled linseed oil so as to form a firm putty. This application contains the acid in too dilute a form to excoriate [irritate] the skin, which it may be made to cover to any extent that may be thought desirable, while its substance serves as a reservoir of the antiseptic material. So long as any discharge continues, the paste should be changed daily, and, in order to prevent the chance of mischief occurring during the process, a piece of rag dipped in the solution of carbolic acid in oil is put on next the skin, and maintained there permanently, care being taken to avoid raising it along with the putty. This rag is always kept in an antiseptic condition from contact with the paste above it, and destroys any germs which may fall upon it during the short time that should alone be allowed to pass in the changing of the dressing. The putty should be in a layer about a quarter of an inch thick, and may be advantageously applied rolled out between two pieces of thin calico, which maintain it in the form of a continuous sheet, which may be wrapped in a moment round the whole circumference of a limb if this be thought desirable, while the putty is prevented by the calico from sticking to the rag which is next the skin. When all discharge has ceased, the use of the paste is discontinued, but the original rag is left adhering to the skin till healing by scabbing is supposed to be complete. I have at present in the hospital a man with severe compound fracture of both bones of the left leg, caused by direct violence, who, after the cessation of the sanious [thin, greenish liquid] discharge under the use of the paste, without a drop of pus appearing, has been treated for the last two weeks exactly as if the fracture was a simple one. During this time the rag, adhering by means of a crust of inspissated [clotted] blood collected beneath it, has continued perfectly dry, and it will be left untouched till the usual period for removing the splints in a simple fracture, when we may fairly expect to find a sound cicatrix [scar] beneath it.

We cannot, however, always calculate on so perfect a result as this. More or less pus may appear after the lapse of the first week, and the larger the wound, the more likely this is to happen. And here I would desire earnestly to enforce the necessity of persevering with the antiseptic application in spite of the appearance of suppuration so long as other symptoms are favorable. The surgeon is extremely apt to suppose that any suppuration is an indication that the antiseptic treatment has failed, and that poulticing or water dressing should be resorted to. But such a course would in many cases sacrifice a limb or a life. I cannot, however, expect my professional brethren to follow my advice blindly in such a matter, and therefore I feel it necessary to place before them, as shortly as I can, some pathological principles intimately connected, not only with the point we are immediately considering, but with the whole subject of this paper.

A Second Method

If a perfectly healthy granulating sore be well washed and covered with a plate of clean metal, such as block tin, fitting its surface pretty accurately, and overlapping the surrounding skin an inch or so in every direction and retained in position by adhesive plaster and a bandage, it will be found, on removing it after twenty-four or forty-eight hours, that little or nothing that can be called pus is present, merely a little transparent fluid, while at the same time there is an entire absence of the unpleasant odour invariably perceived when water dressing is changed. Here the clean metallic surface presents no recesses like those of porous lint for the septic germs to develop in, the fluid exuding from the surface of the granulations has flowed away undecomposed, and the result is the absence of suppuration. This simple experiment illustrates the important fact that granulations have no inherent tendency to form pus, but do so only when subjected to preternatural stimulus. Further, it shows that the mere contact of a foreign body does not of itself stimulate granulations to suppurate; whereas the presence of decomposing organic matter does. These truths are even more strikingly exemplified by the fact that I have elsewhere recorded (*Lancet*, March 23rd, 1867), that a piece of dead bone free from decomposition may not only fail to induce the granulations around it to suppurate, but may actually be absorbed by them; whereas a bit of dead bone soaked with putrid pus infallibly induces suppuration in its vicinity. . . .

Saving a Boy's Arm

I left behind me in Glasgow a boy, thirteen years of age, who, between three and four weeks previously, met with a most severe injury to the left arm, which he got entangled in a machine at a fair. There was a wound six inches long and three inches broad, and the skin was very extensively undermined beyonds its limits, while the soft parts were generally so much lacerated that a pair of dressing forceps [bandage tweezers] introduced at the wound and pushed directly inwards appeared beneath the skin at the opposite aspect of the limb. From this wound several tags of muscle were hanging, and among them was one consisting of about three inches of the triceps [a muscle] in almost its entire thickness; while the lower fragment of the bone, which was broken high up, was protruding four inches and a half, stripped of muscle, the skin being tucked in under it. Without the assistance of the antiseptic treatment, I should certainly have thought of nothing else but amputation at the shoulder-joint; but, as the radial [at the wrist] pulse could be felt and the fingers had sensation, I did not hesitate to try to save the limb and adopted the plan of treatment above described, wrapping the arm from the shoulder to below the elbow in the antiseptic application, the whole interior of the wound, together with the protruding bone, having previously been freely treated with strong carbolic acid. About the tenth day, the discharge, which up to that time had been only sanious and serous [thin and watery] showed a slight admixture of slimy pus; and this increased till (a few days before I left) it amounted to about three drachms [drams] in twenty-four hours. But the boy continued as he had been after the second day, free from unfavorable symptoms, with pulse, tongue, appetite and sleep natural and strength increasing, while the limb remained as it had been from the first, free from swelling, redness, or pain. I, therefore, persevered with the antiseptic dressing; and, before I left, the discharge was already somewhat less, while the bone was becoming firm. I think it likely that, in that boy's case, I should have found merely a superficial sore had I taken off all the dressings at the end of the three weeks; though, considering the extent of the injury, I thought it prudent to let the month expire before disturbing the rag next the skin. But I feel sure that, if I had resorted to ordinary dressing when the pus first appeared, the progress of the case would have been exceedingly different.

Abscesses

The next class of cases to which I have applied the antiseptic treatment is that of abscesses. Here also the results have been extremely satisfactory, and in beautiful harmony with the pathological principles indicated above. The pyogenic membrane [a thin covering that forms over a wound] like the granulations of a sore, which it resembles in nature, forms pus, not from any inherent disposition to do so, but only because it is subjected to some preternatural stimulation. In an ordinary abscess, whether acute or chronic, before it is opened the stimulus which maintains the suppuration is derived from the presence of pus pent up within the cavity. When a free opening is made in the ordinary way, this stimulus is got rid of, but the atmosphere gaining access to the contents, the potent stimulus of decomposition comes into operation, and pus is generated in greater abundance than before. But when the evacuation is effected on the antiseptic principle, the pyogenic membrane, freed from the influence of the former stimulus without the substitution of a new one, ceases to suppurate (like the granulations of a sore under metallic dressing), furnishing merely a trifling amount of clear serum, and, whether the opening be dependent or not, rapidly contracts and coalesces. At the same time any constitutional symptoms previously occasioned by the accumulation of the matter are got rid of without the slightest risk of the irritative or hectic fever hitherto so justly dreaded in dealing with large abscesses.

In order that the treatment may be satisfactory, the abscess must be seen before it is opened. Then, except in very rare and peculiar cases, there are no septic organisms in the contents, so that it is needless to introduce carbolic acid into the interior. Indeed, such a procedure would be objectionable, as it would stimulate the pyogenic membrane to unnecessary suppuration. All that is requisite is to guard against the introduction of living atmospheric germs from without, at the same time that free opportunity is afforded for the escape of the discharge from within. . . .

A Severe Hand Wound

Ordinary contused wounds are, of course, amenable to the same treatment as compound fractures, which are a complicated variety of them. I will content myself with mentioning a single instance of this class of cases. In April last, a volunteer was discharging a rifle when it burst, and blew back the thumb with its metacarpal bone, so that it could be bent back as on a binge at the trapezial joint, which had evidently been opened, while all the soft parts between the metacarpal bones of the thumb and forefinger were torn through. I need not insist before my present audience on the ugly character of such an injury. My house-surgeon, Mr. Hector Cameron, applied carbolic acid to the whole raw surface, and completed the dressing as if for compound fracture. The hand remained free from pain, redness or swelling, and with the exception of a shallow groove, all the wound consolidated without a drop of matter, so that if it had been a clean cut, it would have been regarded as a good example of primary union. The small granulating surface soon healed, and at present a linear cicatrix alone tells of the injury he has sustained, while his thumb has all its movements and his hand a fine grasp.

If the severest forms of contused and lacerated wounds heal thus kindly under the antiseptic treatment, it is obvious that its application to simple incised wounds must be merely a matter of detail. . . .

It would carry me far beyond the limited time which, by the rules of the Association, is alone at my disposal, were I to enter into the various applications of the antiseptic principle in the several special departments of surgery.

Healthier Hospitals

There is, however, one point more that I cannot but advert [refer] to, viz., [that is] the influence of this mode of treatment upon the general healthiness of a hospital. Previously to its introduction the two large wards in which most of my cases of accident and of operation are treated were among the unhealthiest in the whole surgical division of the Glasgow Royal Infirmary, in consequence apparently of those wards being unfavorably placed with reference to the supply of fresh air; and I have felt ashamed when recording the results of my practice, to have so often to allude to hospital gangrene or pyaemia. It was interesting, though melancholy, to observe that whenever all or nearly all the beds contained cases with open sores, these grievous complications were pretty sure to show themselves; so that I came to welcome simple fractures, though in themselves of little interest either for myself or the students, because their presence diminished the proportion of open sores among the patients. But since the antiseptic treatment has been brought into full operation, and wounds and abscesses no longer poison the atmosphere with putrid exhalations, my wards, though in other respects under precisely the same circumstances as before, have completely changed their character; so that during the last nine months not a single instance of pyaemia, hospital gangrene, or erysipelas [types of wound infection] has occurred in them.

As there appears to be no doubt regarding the cause of this change, the importance of the fact can hardly be exaggerated.

Searching for Magic Bullets

By Ernst Bäumler

At the start of the twentieth century, German scientist Paul Ehrlich explored both the body's natural defenses against disease-causing microbes (the immune system) and possible defenses that chemistry might provide in the form of drugs. He coined the term *magic bullet* to refer to any kind of defense that destroyed dangerous elements in the body without harming normal cells. In this selection, Ehrlich biographer Ernst Bäumler (who has also written books in German about cancer and chemistry) shows Ehrlich using the term in a letter to fellow researcher Emil Behring in the spring of 1905. Ehrlich wrote that when the immune system could not provide magic bullets, chemical agents—that is, drugs—should do so. Bäumler says that at this time, Ehrlich focused his drug development efforts on trypanosomes, a group of microorganisms that cause sleeping sickness and several other serious tropical illnesses. He and his coworkers found that several types of dye, as well as some compounds related to the poison arsenic, killed these microorganisms.

In another letter written in early 1905, which Bäumler quotes at length, Ehrlich outlines the process he expects to apply in his search for magic bullets when he takes control of a new research institution in Frankfurt, the Georg Speyer Haus. Ehrlich stresses the importance of testing possible drugs on animals that have been given the disease that the drugs are intended to cure, in order to determine the drugs' effectiveness in the living body as well as their possible danger to the animals. Ehrlich's approach to drug design influenced many later researchers, including those who developed antibiotics. It also led to his discovery of a drug capable of killing the microbes that cause syphilis, a serious sexually transmitted disease, one of the few true magic bullets that existed before antibiotics.

till convinced that serum therapy was the ideal method for contending with infectious diseases, Ehrlich explained [in a letter to fellow scientist Emil Behring], "The antibodies are to some extent magic bullets which seek out their own target without damaging the organism. Consequently, in all circumstances where it is feasible, the immunization method is preferable to any other therapy." Unfortunately, there are many infections in which, for various reasons, the organism does not produce enough "magic bullets" to combat the pathogens. The body's own defense system fails mainly if the pathogens are large ones, like the protozoa that are responsible for malaria and other tropical infections. The situation is similar in the case of sleeping sickness, which had stricken millions of victims among African natives. In these tropical diseases, the pathogens attack the human victims only indirectly, because they first need an intermediate host. For the plasmodia [a type of protozoan] of malaria, this host is a species of mosquito, and for sleeping sickness a species of fly. "In all these cases," wrote Ehrlich, "an attempt must be made to kill the parasites within the body by chemical agents. In other words, chemical agents must be used where serum therapy is impossible." This, Ehrlich explained on another occasion, meant that chemotherapy would have to substitute for serum therapy.

To develop a campaign strategy against armies of parasites, Ehrlich once again turned to his side-chain theory. It must be possible, he argued, to use chemical substances to block the side-chain receptors of microorganisms that have penetrated into the body, whereupon the microorganism would no longer be capable of following the normal course of its metabolism. It would, he concluded, be killed by this "blockade" of its receptors or by the body's own resistance. In Ehrlich's view, every therapeutic or toxic action was based on a localization and fixation of the relevant agent, a phenomenon he described as a "tropism." "Hence," he said, "I call a substance acting on the parasites parasitotropic and substances acting on the organs of the body organotropic. So when a therapeutic substance is injected into an infected organism, it will have to be distributed between the cells of the organism and the parasites, and it will depend only on the nature of this distribution whether a curative effect occurs." Those engaged in chemotherapeutic research, therefore, would have to look for, or produce, compounds with a maximum parasitotropic and minimum organotropic effect. To achieve this it would be necessary to

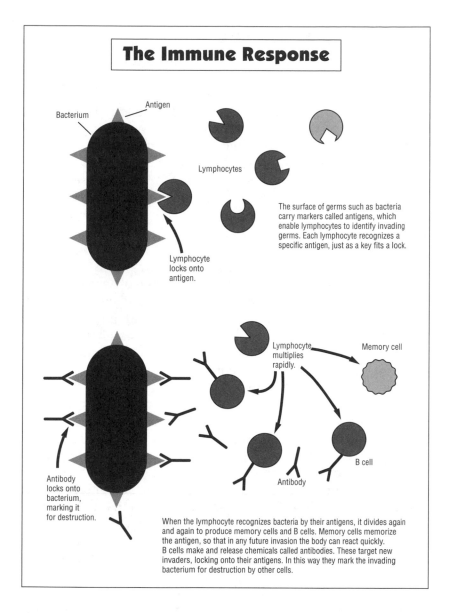

The Immune Response

Bacterium

Antigen

Lymphocytes

Lymphocyte locks onto antigen.

The surface of germs such as bacteria carry markers called antigens, which enable lymphocytes to identify invading germs. Each lymphocyte recognizes a specific antigen, just as a key fits a lock.

Lymphocyte multiplies rapidly.

Memory cell

B cell

Antibody

Antibody locks onto bacterium, marking it for destruction.

When the lymphocyte recognizes bacteria by their antigens, it divides again and again to produce memory cells and B cells. Memory cells memorize the antigen, so that in any future invasion the body can react quickly. B cells make and release chemicals called antibodies. These target new invaders, locking onto their antigens. In this way they mark the invading bacterium for destruction by other cells.

utilize synthetic chemistry, whose task would be to "act by varying the starting substances to a large extent through various types of chemical intervention and to test each of the resulting products for its curative value," in other words, to learn a kind of "chemical targeting." The objects on which Ehrlich decided to try out the action of new compounds were trypanosomes, protozoa only a few hundredths of a millimeter in length.

Tests on Trypanosomes

In 1903, Dr. David Bruce, the British specialist in tropical medicine, had discovered in Uganda that one particular species of those trypanosomes—*Trypanosoma gambiense*—was the cause of sleeping sickness. The pathogens were transmitted from affected victims to the healthy by *Gossina palpalis*, a stinging fly. Trypanosomes were also discovered to be the "perpetrators" of such tropical diseases as nagäna and Chagas' disease. The technique for studying their action was developed by two French researchers, Alphonse Laveran, the "originator of the pathology of protozoa" who had discovered the cause of malaria in 1880 and who was awarded the Nobel Prize in 1907, and F.E.P. Mesnil, the well-known zoologist who had published numerous papers on the subject of parasites. They found that when they transferred trypanosomes from one mouse to another in a drop of subcutaneously [under the skin] injected blood the second mouse died within a few days. The disease progressed in accordance with a fixed pattern, the stages of which could be ascertained very simply with blood tests on the mice, in which the microscopically determinable condition and number of parasites could be found.

Taking their research a step farther, Ehrlich reverted to his old love, dyes, testing the action of the dyes on infected mice. At that time, Ehrlich's most important co-worker was the Japanese bacteriologist Kiyoshi Shiga from the Institute for Infectious Diseases in Tokyo, who had discovered the *Bacillus dysenteriae* [a bacterium that causes severe diarrhea] in Japan in 1898 and who worked at the Frankfurt Institute for Experimental Therapy from May 1901 until 1905. Thus, it was with Shiga that Ehrlich discovered that "trypanosomes react with marked sensitivity to a red dye from the so-called benzopurpurin series. Benzidine dyes of this type can remain in the tissue and blood of the experimental animals for weeks without being excreted." Among the numerous dyes of this class, trypan red was found to have an extremely powerful parasitotropic action; indeed, a number of experimental animals were actually healed with a single injection. Richard Koch, the medical historian from Frankfurt, suggests what this discovery might have been like when he writes: "It must have been a great moment for Paul Ehrlich when he first saw that the mice which had received a deadly dose of trypanosomes were still alive and their blood revealed no more trypanosomes under the microscope."

Once Ehrlich identified the nitrogen-containing azo group in the trypan red compound as the curative atom group, he began looking for other elements related to nitrogen. This brought him to the arsenic compounds.

More Specific Drugs

The use of arsenic was not new. Since the Middle Ages, doctors had been aware not only of how effective but also how dangerous arsenic could be. Furthermore, at the very beginning of this trypanosome research work in 1902, Ehrlich had read an essay on an arsenic compound obtained nearly forty years previously (in 1863) by Pierre Jacques Antoine Béchamp, a French chemist. Moreover, Mesnil and Laveran had already determined that arsenous acid acted on protozoa, and the Vereinigte Chemische Werke Charlottenburg had marketed the slightly modified substance, para-aminophenylarsenic acid, under the name of atoxyl, which Ehrlich and Shiga had used on trypanosomes as early as 1902. Their interest, however, soon ceased, for the strain of trypanosomes that they tried out did not react to atoxyl. What Ehrlich and Shiga could not have known at that time was that it was arsenic resistant.

As a result, Shiga and Ehrlich resumed work on the action of dye compounds against parasites, while the French researchers F.E.P. Mesnil and Charles Nicolle developed trypan blue. This was used to combat piroplasmosis, an animal disease caused by protozoa.

The benzidine dyes were followed by another dye class—the triphenyl methane dyes. These included malachite green, which some researchers claimed to be effective against trypanosome infections. Ehrlich and his co-workers were particularly interested in parafuchsine and tryparosan, both dyes which killed the trypanosomes rapidly. . . .

Ehrlich set out in detail the objectives he proposed to follow in the new institute [the Georg Speyer Haus] in a letter to Professor [Ludwig] Darmstaedter dated January 4, 1905, which provides so much insight into Ehrlich's work and thought at that time, it is reproduced here, only slightly abridged:

> As you are aware, in most pharmacological institutes . . . preference is given to pursuing purely theoretical science, aimed chiefly at determining the mode of action of the toxins (toxicology). It is only natural that the substances researched in the first place are ones (especially alkaloids) that produce interesting and significant

toxic effects. However, the majority of such highly toxic substances (if one excludes a few alkaloids such as morphine, cocaine, atropine, etc.) are not suitable for sickbed use. . . .

On the other hand, our best established pharmaceuticals (such as potassium iodide, mercury, etc.) receive insufficient scientific attention. At most, one discovers how toxic the relevant substances are that kill the animals, but the factors that enable the relevant substances to heal a certain disease continue to be veiled in obscurity and are bound to remain so with this working method.

When we note, for example, that iodine preparations or mercury preparations in doses virtually harmless to the organism and its cells cause absorption of certain disease products in a specific manner, it is obvious from the simplest consideration that this specific therapeutic action can be scientifically analyzed only if experimental animals can be inoculated with the relevant diseases and experimented upon.

Experiments on normal animals like those employed almost exclusively in pharmacology are quite meaningless in this vitally important question, for all we learn from them are the hazards that accompany excessive dosages of the relevant substances (e.g. mercury).

Ehrlich conceded that this aspect did, of course, have some importance as one way of helping "to avoid harmful side effects and poisoning of the patient, because we know which early symptoms of intolerance we have to look for." Yet that, in his view, was of no particularly great benefit,

since we try to chart the course of therapy in such a way as to avoid the sandbanks of injury completely. One can, indeed, be grateful to the men who have given protection against the hazards of putting to sea between the beacons of poisoning, but they have not plotted the course out into the open sea of healing.

In particular, let me emphasize that I consider "pure" toxicology a thoroughly justified and necessary science, and the same holds good for biology and physiology, which have been of the utmost importance as the basis of our medical insight. I dispute only that practical therapeutics have benefited from it to a corresponding degree.

A glance at the drugs then available bore out this assertion:

> The best that we possess were discovered by trial and error (e.g.,
> quinine, potassium iodide, mercury, opium, digitalis), whereas the
> vast number of recent synthetic medicines derive primarily from
> the initiative of our chemical industry. The pharmacologists here
> have assumed only the modest role of providing the service of
> eliminating anything, with very few exceptions . . ., too toxic from
> the enormous number of preparations and handing over to the
> medical practitioners those remaining which appeared likely to be
> of therapeutic use. . . .

> In addition, anyone surveying the vast array of recent drugs and
> feeling gratified that we now have valuable antipyretics [drugs to
> reduce fever], soporifics [drugs to induce sleep] and antiseptics,
> cannot avoid certain misgivings about the general direction of
> progress. Notwithstanding decades of hard work and the output of
> thousands of intellects, all we have achieved have been sympto-
> matics [drugs that ease symptoms of illness] but not true thera-
> peutic agents like quinine against malaria. Yet this is the ultimate
> objective of all medical art.

A Focus on Chemistry

There was not the slightest doubt in Ehrlich's mind how this ob-
jective would be achieved:

> A therapeutic agent for a particular disease can be discovered only
> in an organism suffering from that disease. For many reasons,
> however, (humanitarian considerations and the technique of sci-
> entific experimentation), the sick patient is a highly unsuitable sub-
> ject to use in the discovery of medicines. Attention is not focused
> on the patient until the drug has been recognized as effective in an
> extensive series of experiments in animals. Hence, it is essential
> for specified diseases to be produced experimentally so that the
> experiments can be conducted upon them.

> Of course, this is easiest in the case of infectious diseases. Indeed,
> the greatest successes have already been achieved in this way. . . . I
> would mention here only [Robert] Koch's tuberculin [a drug used
> at the time to treat tuberculosis] work and the wonderful discovery
> of the local tuberculin reaction, then [Emil] Behring's discovery of

the antitoxins with their wide ramifications through the entire field
of infectious diseases. . . . [The principle is] naturally not restricted
to the infectious diseases, but generally valid, as witness the treatment of myxoedema and cretinism [diseases caused by poor thyroid
function] by thyroid gland preparations. I now believe that the field
of experimental therapy is—perhaps contrary to appearances—not
limited to the use of curative agents which, like antitoxins and tox-
ins, are the products of living cells. Rather, I believe that synthetic
chemicals can also be very useful in this line of approach.

Ehrlich was thinking here primarily of the many major diseases,
those like malaria and trypanosomiases that are due to protozoa
and those like smallpox, foot-and-mouth disease, cattle plague and
syphilis that are due to pathogenic organisms [then] of an unknown kind. He continued:

In some of these diseases (malaria and trypanosomiases, for example), the immune response and its use play a minor part from the
curative viewpoint. On the other hand, in some cases the organisms
causing the disease seem capable of being killed entirely within the
living subject by chemical agents, so that complete disinfection of
the infected organism—i.e., the cure—is both possible and practi-
cable. I would mention here merely the cure of malaria by quinine
and that of certain trypanosome infections by a dye discovered by
myself (trypan red). The trypanosome diseases in particular play a
very important part in that they include one of the most widespread
animal diseases in the tropical regions. In addition, sleeping sickness, which occurs in central Africa—in Uganda—and decimates
the population there, is due to the same parasite.

I already believe that trypan red in combination with arsenic based
on Laveran's experiments will perform far more effectively than
all other agents used previously. I must, however, attempt to discover a still better curative agent. Hitherto, I have investigated
about twenty new and very hard-to-produce preparations without
the desired result. But what does this number signify compared
with the 100-fold possibilities of new dye combinations which are
feasible here?

The salient point of crucial importance to this type of experimental therapy . . . [is] the production of the numerous preparations
necessary for a good final result. However, very many compounds

have to be newly produced in stages in accordance with a specific plan if anything is to be achieved. I have tried to introduce amido groups, sulpho radicals, etc., into trypan red in certain positions and thereby improve its efficacy.

Dr. Arthur Weinberg was eager—purely out of interest—to lend his support so that my wishes could be met. However, I was unable to take advantage of this great kindness without making excessive demands, as that would have required an entire laboratory.

I encountered the same difficulties earlier, when, in methylene blue [a dye] I found an agent that acted on malaria similarly to quinine, although not so reliably. Even so, with certain forms [of malaria] (blackwater level) on which quinine has a toxic action, it is useful to have an alternative agent available. At that time, however, I could not work out the stages of the synthesis to locate the improvement for the unrelated reason that I had no chemical assistant; so this basically important matter was not followed up.

Those are only two examples from my own experience. I think the field of experimental chemical therapy will expand increasingly in the future, but that expansion will be encouragingly rapid only if the researcher in charge is relieved of the difficulties of material procurement and not forced to rely on chance favors. Ideally, this is achievable only if a special chemical laboratory is attached to the medical institute and in the charge of a dynamic organic chemist who, together with one or two assistants, can take over the purely chemical aspects of the work and, with his greater experience, encourage the chemical enterprise of the medical practitioner involved.

In my opinion, a combination like that suggested here meets a real requirement of medical research, and I do not doubt that this could achieve much for the benefit and well-being of the sick and would certainly lead to an expansion of our therapeutic expertise and the discovery of 'genuine' curative agents.

I am therefore convinced that the establishment of such an institute in the Speyer Haus would best accord with the generous intentions in the donors' minds and, consequently, I have no misgivings—so far as the interests of my scientific work are concerned—in endorsing this plan most warmly.

CHAPTER 2

The Discovery of Antibiotics

Alexander Fleming Discovers Penicillin

By André Maurois

In this selection, French writer André Maurois, known for his bi-ographies of literary figures such as Victor Hugo and George Sand, describes the historic moment in 1928 when Scottish-born bacteriologist Alexander Fleming, walking around his London laboratory with a visitor, looked at a discarded dish in his sink and said "That's funny. . . ." Maurois explains that the dish contained colonies of staphylococci, a type of bacteria that causes dangerous wound infections. A speck of mold had blown onto the dish, and Fleming noticed that the area around the mold was clear—no bacteria were growing there. The arrival of the mold was a piece of luck, but Maurois stresses that Fleming was prepared to understand its significance because the scientist had already been looking for a substance that could kill microorganisms in the blood without harming living things.

Maurois writes that Merlin Pryce, Fleming's visitor, reported that Fleming immediately took steps to preserve the dish and the mold. According to Maurois, Fleming went on to grow the mold, study the effects on bacteria of the golden liquid the mold produced, and ask experts to help him identify it. It proved to belong to the *Penicillium* family. Fleming concluded, Maurois says, that the "mould juice" was an example of antibiosis, in which one type of organism produces a substance to kill other types in order to give itself an advantage in evolutionary competition. Maurois lists earlier scientists, including Louis Pasteur, who had also observed antibiosis, but he notes that all antibiotic compounds had so far proved poisonous to humans as well as bacteria. He states that few scientists of Fleming's time believed that such a compound could ever become a useful drug, but Fleming hoped that his "mould juice" (which he named penicillin) would prove to be an exception and decided to investigate it further.

I n most of the great scientific discoveries there has been one part deliberate research and one part luck. Pasteur, a man of unusual firmness of purpose who sought the truth with a combination of pure reason and experiment, was sometimes helped by Chance. He was called upon to deal with *ad hoc* problems which later were to lead him to general conclusions. If he had not been appointed to a professorship at Lille, if the distillers and brewers of the neighbourhood had not gone to him for advice, he might perhaps not have come to take an interest in fermentations, though, his genius being what it was, he would have discovered something else. Fleming had for a long time been hunting for a substance which should be able to kill the pathogenic microbes without damage to the patient's cells. Pure chance deposited this substance on his bench. But, had he not been waiting for fifteen years, he would not have recognized the unknown visitor for what it was.

Killing Germs Inside the Body

Once again [in 1928], as at the very beginning of his career, he had just been taking stock of the weapons which medicine could employ against the infections. The means of defence were woefully inadequate but he refused to give up hope. 'At present', he wrote, 'there seems little chance of finding any general antiseptic capable of killing bacteria in the blood stream, though there is some hope that chemicals may be produced with special affinities for special bacteria which may be able to destroy these in the blood, although they may be quite without action on other and, it may be, closely allied bacteria.'

He was studying a new antiseptic, mercuric chloride, which killed streptococci, though, as always, at a degree of concentration which the human body could not tolerate. He put the question to himself whether, by injecting it into the blood stream in weaker doses, it might not be possible to achieve a degree of concentration which would not destroy either the human cells or the streptococci, but *might* have the effect of making the latter more fragile and, consequently, more vulnerable to the action of the phagocytes.

His laboratory was still small and encumbered. An accumulation of culture dishes was piled in apparent disorder, though he could always find the one he wanted without a moment's hesitation. His door was almost always left open and any young research-worker in need of some variety of microbe or of some particular implement was given a warm welcome. Fleming would stretch out an arm, lay his hand at once on the required culture, give it to the intruder, and then, usually without uttering a word, go back to his work. When the air in the tiny room became stifling he would open the window which looked on to Praed Street [in London].

In 1928 he agreed to contribute an article on the staphylococci to a vast undertaking—*A System of Bacteriology*—to be published by the Medical Research Council. Some time before this, his colleague, Merlin Pryce (now Professor Pryce) had, while working with him, devoted a certain amount of study to some abnormal forms, mutants, of these microbes.

Fleming, who liked nothing better than to give a helping hand to the young, wanted to quote Pryce in his article. But the latter had left [Almroth] Wright's department [where Fleming worked] before he could complete his researches. Being a conscientious scientist he did not want to publish his results without verifying them, and his new job gave him insufficient leisure in which to do this quickly. Fleming, therefore, had to work again over the ground already covered by Pryce, and set himself to study numerous colonies of staphylococci. In order to examine these colonies, cultivated on agar in Petri dishes, he had to lift the lids of the dishes and leave the contents for some considerable time exposed under the microscope, which meant running a risk of contamination.

'That's Funny . . .'

Pryce went to see Fleming in his little laboratory, where he found him, as usual, surrounded by innumerable dishes. The cautious Scot disliked being separated from his cultures before he was quite certain that there was no longer anything to be learned from them. He was often teased about his disorderly habits. He was now to prove that disorder may have its uses. With his rough humour he reproached Pryce for obliging him to re-do a long job of work, and, while speaking, took up several old cultures and removed the lids. Several of the cultures had been contaminated with mould—a not unusual occurrence. 'As soon as you uncover a culture dish something tiresome is sure to happen. Things fall out of the air.'

Suddenly, he stopped talking, then, after a moment's observation, said, in his usual unconcerned tones: 'That's funny . . .' On the culture at which he was looking there was a growth of mould, as on several of the others, but on this particular one, all round the mould, the colonies of staphylococci had been dissolved and, instead of forming opaque yellow masses, looked like drops of dew.

Pryce had often seen old microbial colonies which for various reasons had dissolved. He thought that probably the mould was producing acids which were harmful to the staphylococci—no unusual occurrence. But, noticing the keen interest with which Fleming was examining the phenomenon, he said: 'That's how you discovered lysozyme.' Fleming made no answer. He was busy taking a little piece of the mould with his scalpel, and putting it in a tube of broth. Then he picked off a scrap measuring about one square millimetre, which floated on the surface of the broth. He obviously wanted to make quite sure that this mysterious mould would be preserved.

From Observation to Action

'What struck me', Pryce says, 'was that he didn't confine himself to observing, but took action at once. Lots of people observe a phenomenon, feeling that it may be important, but they don't get beyond being surprised—after which, they forget. That was never the case with Fleming. I remember another incident, also from the time when I was working with him. One of my cultures had not been successful, and he told me to be sure of getting everything possible out of my mistakes. That was characteristic of his whole attitude to life.'

Fleming put the Petri dish aside. He was to keep it as a precious treasure for the rest of his life. He showed it to one of his colleagues: 'Take a look at that,' he said, 'it's interesting—the kind of thing I like; it may well turn out to be important.' The colleague in question looked at the dish, then handed it back with a polite: 'Yes, very interesting.' But Fleming, in no way discouraged by this manifestation of indifference, temporarily abandoned his investigation of the staphylococci, and gave himself entirely to studying the surprising mould.

What exactly is a mould? It is one of those tiny fungi, green, brown, yellow or black, which proliferate in damp cupboards or on old boots. This type of vegetation results from 'spores'— smaller than a red blood corpuscle—reproductive organs which float in the air. When one of them settles upon a suitable medium, it germinates, buds and puts out shoots in every direction until a soft mass forms.

Fleming transferred several spores to a dish containing agar and left them for four or five days to germinate at room temperature. He soon obtained a colony of the mould similar to the first one. Then he planted in the same agar different bacteria in isolated streaks, forming, as it were, the radii of a circle with the mould as centre. After incubation, he noticed that certain microbes survived in close proximity to the fungus—the streptococci, the staphylococci and the diphtheria bacillus, for instance, whereas the typhoid and influenza bacilli were not affected in the same way.

The discovery was becoming tremendously interesting. Unlike lysozyme, which acted more especially upon the inoffensive microbes, this mould seemed to produce a substance which could inhibit the growth of microbes which caused some of the most serious diseases. It might, therefore, have an immense therapeutic value. 'Here,' said Fleming, 'it looks as though we have got a mould that can do something useful.' He cultivated his *penicillium* in a larger receptacle containing a nutritive broth. A thick, soft, pock-marked mass, at first white, then green, then black, covered the surface. At first the broth remained clear. After several days the liquid assumed a vivid yellow colour. What mattered now was to find out whether this liquid also possessed the bactericidal properties of the mould.

The methods perfected in 1922 for lysozyme suited Fleming's purpose admirably. He hollowed out a gutter in a dish of agar and filled it with a mixture of agar and the yellow liquid. Then microbes were planted in streaks, perpendicularly to the gutter, up to the very edge of the dish. The liquid appeared to be just as active as the original mould. The same microbes were affected. There was therefore in the broth a bactericidal (or bacteriostatic) substance produced by the mould. How great a strength did it have? Fleming experimented with weaker and weaker solutions—a 20th, a 40th, a 200th, a 500th. Even this last still arrested the development of the staphylococci. The mysterious substance contained in the golden liquid appeared to be endowed with quite extraordinary power. Fleming at that time had no means of knowing that the proportion of the active substance in the 'juice' was scarcely more than one in a million. The proportion of gold in the sea is greater than that.

What Mould Is It?

It was important now to identify the mould. There are thousands of moulds. Fleming's knowledge of mycology (the science of fungi) was no more than elementary. He turned to his books, rummaged about in them, and decided that the substance in question was a penicillium of the genus *chrysogenum*. There happened just then to be at St. Mary's [Hospital, where Fleming worked,] a young Irish mycologist, C.J. La Touche, who was assisting [John] Freeman in his researches into asthma. Freeman had got hold of him because a Dutch research-worker had put forward the theory that many cases of asthma among those living in damp rooms were due to moulds. La Touche was a sensitive individual who found the restless atmosphere of the Inoculation Department little to his liking. But he had made his colleagues aware of the importance of moulds, and they had affectionately nicknamed him 'Old Mouldy'.

Fleming showed his fungus to La Touche who, after studying it, decided that it was the *penicillium rubrum*. The bacteriologist deferred to the expert and in his first paper on the subject gave to his mould the name prescribed by La Touche. Two years later, the famous American mycologist, [Charles] Thom, identified the fungus as a *penicillium notatum* (close to the *chrysogenum* which had been Fleming's first diagnosis). La Touche very graciously wrote to Fleming, apologizing for having misled him. Fleming learned from Thom's book that the *penicillium notatum* had been originally recognized by a Swedish chemist, [Richard] Westling, on a specimen of decayed hyssop [an herb of the mint family]. This reminded Fleming the Covenanter [Scottish Presbyterian] of Psalm 51: 'Purge me with hyssop and I shall be clean'—the first known reference to penicillin.

Microbe Wars

Meanwhile, his experiments on the bactericidal action of the liquid had convinced him that he was in the presence of a phenomenon of antibiosis. The mould, a rudimentary living creature, produced a substance which killed other living creatures, microbes. The peaceful co-existence of the two species was not possible.

That living creatures could be caught up in a vital and murderous struggle, the spectacle presented by the world had always proved. They squabble over food, air and living-space. Sometimes they complement each other, the one providing what the other lacks, and, when that happens, a shared life, a 'symbiosis' is possible. More often, however, proximity is fatal to one of them. In 1889 the Frenchman, [Jean-Antoine] Vuillemin, had for the first time employed the word 'antibiosis', defining it thus: 'When two living bodies are closely united, and one of the two exercises a destructive action on a more or less extensive portion of the other, then we can say that "antibiosis" exists.'

A striking example is that of all the infectious microbes which are ceaselessly being emptied into water and soil. Most of them do not survive, and this must needs be so, since, otherwise, neither men nor animals could live at all. What is it that destroys these microbes? To a very great extent, the sun, but also the action of other microbes which are inoffensive, or even beneficial, to human beings. There are ancient Greek texts which point out that certain epidemics cause the disappearance of other ailments.

Early Observations

In [Joseph] Lister's Commonplace-Books [notebooks] (now in the library of the Royal College of Surgeons), we find under the date November 25th, 1871, the following observation: in a glass tube containing urine, Lister noticed the presence of numerous bacteria, but also of some granular filaments which he recognized as mould. Seeing that the bacteria seemed to be in poor condition, he made several experiments for the purpose of determining whether the growth of mould had the effect of making the liquid an unfavourable medium for bacteria. These experiments were inconclusive and he abandoned them. But he had noted that the presence of a soft mass (which he thought was *penicillium glaucum*) on the surface of the tube 'was making the bacteria completely immobile and languid'. He supposed that what was happening was a competitive struggle for oxygen, the penicillium absorbing that contained in the broth and blocking the surface.

In 1877, Pasteur and [Jules-François] Joubert had noticed that the anthrax bacillus, when injected at the same time as inoffensive bacteria, produces no infection of the animal. There, again, an antagonism is set up, and the anthrax bacillus is vanquished. 'In the inferior organisms,' Pasteur wrote, 'still more than in the great animal and vegetable species, life hinders life. A liquid invaded by an organized ferment, or by an aerobe [certain types of bacteria] makes it difficult for an inferior organism to multiply . . .' Farther on, having pointed out that a common bacterium introduced into urine at the same time as the bacterium of anthrax prevents the development of the latter, he adds: 'It is a remarkable thing that this same phenomenon occurs in the bodies of those animals which are most prone to contract anthrax, and we are led to the surprising conclusion that one can introduce a profusion of the anthrax bacterium into an animal without the latter contracting the disease; all that is needed is to add common bacteria to the liquid which holds the bacterium of anthrax in suspension. These facts may, perhaps, justify the greatest hopes from the therapeutic point of view.'

In 1897, Dr Duchesne, of Lyon, gave to his thesis (inspired by Professor Gabriel Roux) the title: *Contribution à l'étude de la concurrence vitale chez les micro-organismes. Antagonisme entre les moisissures et les microbes.* 'It is to be hoped', he concluded, 'that if we pursue the study of biological rivalry between moulds and microbes, we may, perhaps, succeed in discovering still other facts which may be directly applicable to therapeutic science.' In this case, too, the search was not continued.

A Flicker of Hope

We see, therefore, that antibiosis was already a known phenomenon. But in 1928 the 'climate' of the scientific world was not favourable to research along those lines. In fact, the reverse is true. All former experiments had demonstrated that every substance fatal to microbes *also* destroyed the tissues of the human body. This seemed almost self-evident. Why should a substance which was poisonous for certain living cells *not* be so, as well, for others, no less delicate?

'The fact', said Fleming, 'that bacterial antagonisms were so common and well known hindered rather than helped the initiation of the study of antibiotics as we know it today.' Such facts no longer produced the least excitement, and gave birth to no hope of a new therapeutic development. More especially was the atmosphere hostile in Wright's department. The Chief was convinced that the only means of helping the natural defences of the body was still immunization. Fleming himself had shown by a brilliant series of experiments that all the antiseptics had proved abortive. He had discovered a natural defence, till then unknown—lysozyme. He had tried to increase its concentration in the blood, but without success. Outside the world of the greater parasites (trypanosomes, spirochaetes), Paul Ehrlich's 'magic bullet' remained a dream. Wright could say again, as he had said in 1912, that 'the chemotherapy of human bacterial infections will never be possible . . .'

Fleming, an observer without preconceived ideas, did, however, see a flicker of hope in his 'mould juice'. Might not the substance for which he had been looking all through his working life be found there? Though that distant flicker was, as yet, feeble, he decided to neglect nothing which might enable him to achieve success. He gave up all other work to concentrate on this research.

Gerhard Domagk Discovers the Sulfa Drugs

By Sebastian G.B. Amyes

Difficulty in growing the *Penicillium* mold and other problems made Alexander Fleming abandon his research on penicillin after a year or two, but in the 1930s, other scientists were also searching for bacteria-killing "magic bullets." One was Gerhard Domagk, a researcher at a large German dye company that, following Paul Ehrlich's lead, was trying to find dyes that could also be used as drugs. As Sebastian G.B. Amyes, a scientist in the department of medical microbiology at the University of Edinburgh (Scotland), explains in this selection, Domagk decided to look for drugs that would kill or weaken *Streptococcus*, which caused several kinds of serious infection.

Amyes describes Domagk's work with a red dye called Prontosil, which began in 1932. Prontosil proved effective not only in mice but in humans, Amyes reports. It saved lives that otherwise would have been lost to infection, including those of Domagk's own daughter and the son of the president of the United States. The dye company hoped to patent the drug, says Amyes, but soon after Domagk reported its success in 1935, French scientists showed that Prontosil's active ingredient was sulfanilamide, a compound that had been discovered much earlier and thus could not be patented. Amyes writes that Domagk and the company then set out to develop a family of related compounds, which became the sulfonamides, or sulfa drugs. Although not strictly antibiotics, these drugs were effective against a number of types of bacteria, just as antibiotics would be. Domagk won a Nobel Prize for his work in 1939, but, Amyes reports, Germany's Nazi government forced him to turn it down.

Sebastian G.B. Amyes, *Magic Bullets, Lost Horizons: The Rise and Fall of Antibiotics*. London: Taylor & Francis, 2001. Copyright © 2001 by Taylor & Francis. Reproduced by permission of the publisher and the author.

Gerhard Domagk, a German from the Brandenburg district, was just 23 at the signing of the armistice [that ended World War I] in November 1918. He had been an infantryman and was wounded in the head in the trenches on the Russian front in 1915. He had been sent back to hospital in Berlin. While he was recuperating, Domagk trained as a medical assistant and was sent back to the Eastern front to work in the battle hospitals. He was horrified by what he saw and recognised that most deaths did not come from direct war injuries but rather from the festering of wounds. This experience made Domagk a life-long pacifist and convinced him that his vocation should be that of a doctor. Within a month of the armistice, Domagk had started his medical studies in the University of Kiel. After graduation, Domagk was appointed as an assistant in the Pathological Institute under the dictatorship of Walter Gross. Gross had been interested in how the body fought off serious infection and Domagk was directed to observe how the blood dealt with bacterial invasion. Domagk noticed that the injection of mice with *Staphylococcus aureus* initiated a migration of killer cells in the blood that met and then engulfed the invader, known as phagocytosis. He demonstrated that if the animal had first been immunised against the bacterium, the number of killer cells was greatly increased. His most important observation was if the bacterium was disabled or damaged in some way, this phagocystic process went into over drive and these cells engulfed the debris. These cells were part of the body's defence system to remove foreign matter from the blood. Domagk speculated that if the system was more efficient with damaged bacteria, all that therapy would have to achieve was to injure the infectious bacterium, and the body would then readily clear the infection. [Heinrich] Horlein was fascinated by Domagk's observations and recruited him to work in his experimental pathology laboratory at I.G. Farbenindustrie in 1927.

Focusing on Streptococcus

The experimental chemical laboratory was enjoying some success. [Wilhelm] Roehl had built on his discovery of Germanin [a chemical that cured sleeping sickness] to produce an anti-malarial drug, plasmoquine, which was much more potent than the only available therapy, quinine. The drug came to market in 1929, at the very time that Roehl developed a carbuncle on his neck and died at the early age of 48. It was ironic that he should have succumbed to a bacterial infection, one of the few organisms to which I.G. Farbenindustrie had not found a potential chemical cure. Domagk was given the freedom to research into whatever he thought was important and he made the decision to ignore all bacteria except the one that had killed Roehl, *Streptococcus*. This bacterium was responsible for a myriad of infections, many of such severity that infection resulted in death or serious disability. In particular it caused both scarlet and rheumatic fever. This highly infectious bacterium was able to invade and damage the heart valves, the kidneys and the liver. Domagk knew that he would have to set up a large systematic search for a chemical that could have the suitable selectivity against the pathogen needed for widespread clinical use. He felt that the limitations of Ehrlich's studies were that the drugs he devised were not tested on a sufficiently rigorous model, so he devised his own. He isolated the most virulent strain of *Streptococcus* he could find, one that had caused rapid, fatal blood-poisoning in a patient from a nearby hospital. He argued that testing of new chemicals in the test-tube might give a false impression of their strength because, as he had already noticed, blood contained cells that could dispose of damaged cells. Therefore, how much more effective it would be to test his new compounds in an animal model; this would be a much more sensitive indicator to the power of these chemicals as he would be measuring not just the ability of the tested compound to inhibit the growth of the *Streptococcus*, as he would in a test-tube, but also the capability of the host to capitalise on this damage and remove the injured bacterial cells. This was a revolutionary concept because maintaining the *Streptococcus* in an animal model also preserved its virulence; it is a strange fact that when most bacteria are cultured successively in artificial laboratory media outside an animal host, they can often rapidly lose their pathogenic characters.

Testing New Drugs

Josef Klarer was the chemist given the task of synthesising the new compounds, while Domagk injected them into mice that had previously been infected with the *Streptococcus*. Klarer concentrated his efforts on the dyes that Roehl had previously examined to cure sleeping sickness. As Roehl had done before him, Klarer altered these compounds little by little. He provided Domagk with

300 new chemicals to inject into his infected mice, but none of them were effective. At the end of 1932, Klarer gave Domagk a new red dye to test. Klarer was pessimistic about its success but Domagk insisted that it should be tested in his animal model. The dye, which Klarer had called KL-730, was injected into infected mice under exactly the same protocol as all its predecessors. After the same period of time when all the mice had died in the previous experiments, Domagk found that all the mice treated with the drug were very much alive and were showing no symptoms of infection. Perhaps the mice had not been infected sufficiently with the *Streptococcus* or the bacterium had lost its virulence? However, Domagk had also infected a control set at mice, which were not treated with the dye and every single mouse in this group was dead. Domagk and his colleagues immediately took sections of tissue from the surviving mice and examined them for the presence of the found bacterial cells, which formed long chains so characteristic of the *Streptococcus*. Under the microscope, he found the organs of the untreated mice to be saturated with live bacteria but he could find no evidence of any intact bacterial cells in the organs of the treated mice. The drug was called Prontosil rubrum but is generally just referred to as Prontosil. Domagk had been prepared for this discovery because of the testing protocol that he had devised. He was not interested in the results in the test tube, only in the capability to cure infection in the intact animal. If the failure of Prontosil to show any antibacterial activity during the laboratory testing had been acceded to, then the discovery would never have been made, In fact, a number of antibacterial drugs are relatively ineffective in the laboratory; they have to be metabolised by the host to release an active component.

Domagk tried his new drug against all types of infection but he quickly noticed that it was ineffective against gram-negative bacteria and was more effective against some gram-positive bacteria than others. It was, however, always exquisitely active against the *Streptococcus*. It was readily absorbed in the gut after being taken by mouth, so the drug survived the barrier of stomach acid. It was also freely excreted through the urine; the body could tolerate and did not accumulate it. To improve the solubility, the drug was prepared as a sodium salt and was available for human trials.

These trials started at the Municipal hospital in Wuppertal under the clinical guidance of Dr. Philipp Klee. An 18-year-old girl was admitted to the hospital suffering from a severe sore throat, caused by *Streptococcus pyogenes*. Within two days, a severe fever started and the bacterium had caused large abscesses behind her tonsils. These were lanced and the fever subsided. However, the fever returned and she had acute nephritis, a severe condition which results in almost complete blockage of the kidneys and a subsequent failure to produce urine. This condition was invariably fatal. Klee treated the girl with regular intravenous [injected into a vein] Prontosil injections. Within 24 hours, the patient's temperature was normal and urine was passed freely. The course continued for a further six days and the patient was eventually discharged completely cured.

Prontosil had been discovered in the laboratories of a large industrial company, which was given to be unwilling to disclose its discovery until it was certain that the drug was effective and safe. Too many miraculous cures had been heralded and late found to be too toxic. Prontosil underwent clinical trials at the Wuppertal

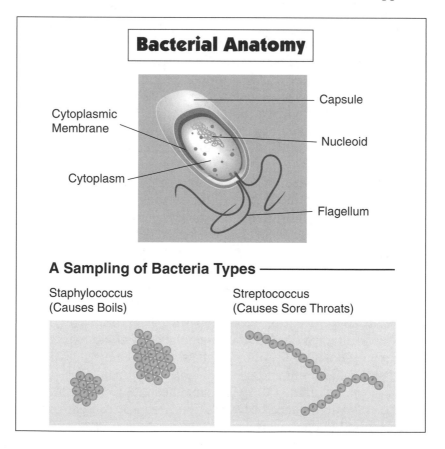

Bacterial Anatomy

Capsule

Cytoplasmic Membrane

Nucleoid

Cytoplasm

Flagellum

A Sampling of Bacteria Types

Staphylococcus
(Causes Boils)

Streptococcus
(Causes Sore Throats)

hospital for two years. Many infections, once fatal, were suddenly curable but they were largely those caused by *Streptococcus* and the related gram-positive bacterium *Staphylococcus*. Nevertheless, the clinical trials demonstrated objectively that Prontosil was an effective treatment for some bacterial infections and Domagk published his results for the first time in 1935.

Prontosil was not readily accepted throughout the world; for some reason Domagk's results were treated with much speculation. Perhaps it was because he was reporting from a chemical company; patent medicines were widespread and it might be that the medical profession considered that this was just yet one more. Some three months after Domagk's initial report, Prontosil was used for the first time to treat a patient in the United States. The woman had bacteriaemia, an infection of the blood caused by *Staphylococcus aureus*, and she was on the point of death. Her family had read of this miracle cure from Germany and insisted that she be treated with Prontosil. Her physicians were openly hostile to the idea but complied. She recovered, although her physicians never attributed her startling improvement to the drug. In England, the drug was first used by Leonard Colebrooke, working at Queen Charlotte's maternity hospital. [Ignaz] Semmelweiss had been overwhelmed by rampant infections in recent mothers, and had tried to take preventative measures [in 1847]; however, here in one of the most modern hospitals of the time, nearly one hundred years later and approaching the middle of the twentieth century, the problem was not significantly better. Colebrooke had no weapons against these sudden and often fatal bouts of infection. He had tried salvarsen, Ehrlich's drug, which apart from having extreme side-effects was not very effective and two-thirds of the patients that he treated still died. In 1936, he treated 38 infected mothers with Prontosil and 35 survived. When further groups of patients were treated, the proportion of successful cures increased to 100%. Prontosil could be completely successful if given early enough once symptoms were developing and could still be effective even in the previously premortal stages of infection.

Dramatic Cures

Domagk's own daughter, Hildegaard, pricked herself in the hand and the wound became infected by *Streptococcus*. Her whole arm showed signs of inflammation and she was rushed to hospital. The bacteria entered the blood and the hospital recommended amputation of the inflamed limb, which was conventional treatment at the time for such infections. Domagk, whose faith in Prontosil was absolute, treated his own daughter and she made a complete recovery. It was, however, Prontosil's success in curing the child of another famous father that guaranteed universal acceptance of Domagk's discovery. In late 1936, the son of the President of the United States, also called Franklin D. Roosevelt, had developed severe tonsillitis and the infection was beginning to spread. Eleanor Roosevelt remained by her son's bedside, convinced that death was imminent. As his fever increased, his doctor tried Prontosil as a final desperate measure. FDR junior made a spectacular recovery and the press hailed the miracle drug; the headline of the *New York Times* read "New Control for Infections". When the Roosevelts' doctors were interviewed they were cautious about the role of Prontosil in this most public of successes, and the press picked this up and stated how American physicians were unenthusiastic about the drug but still rushed to use it.

The Key Compound

Prontosil was patented by I.G. Farbenindustrie but then, as now, competitors sought ways to "bust" the patent. Jacques and Thérèse Tréfouël, with their colleagues Frederick Nitti and Daniel Bovet, manufactured Prontosil in their own laboratory in France. They proved that the active component was not the red dye at all; the compound was metabolised by the body's own enzymes and broken down to a colourless constituent. This constituent was active in the test-tube where Prontosil was not. It was identified as sulphanilamide, the first of the sulphonamides. The irony of the French discovery was that sulphanilamide had been manufactured back in 1909 in the University of Vienna but, of course, had never been tested against bacterial infections. Instead it was patented for use in the manufacture of dyes by a chemical company, I.G. Farbenindustrie! By the time the French discovery was published the patent on sulphanilamide had long expired so could be manufactured by anyone who had the resources to synthesise it. Pure sulphanilamide was used in preference to Prontosil, as it was less unpleasant to take. So I.G. Farbenindustrie was unable to profit from its pioneering investment. However, the company did take part in a race to find other sulphonamides that could inhibit bacterial infections that Prontosil and sulphanilamide had been unable to control. Until the world went back to war in 1939, the most wanted prize was a cure for tuberculosis. Sulphanilamide had stopped the spread of tuberculosis in guinea pigs but only when given in the very highest doses. It was not penetrating the protective cell wall of this most elusive of bacteria. Domagk persuaded his chemists to manufacture a myriad of sulphonamide compounds, which he then tested on the tubercule bacillus. At the very time that Hitler annexed Czechoslovakia in March 1939, one of Domagk's sulphonamides, sulphathiazole, was demonstrated to be much more effective than the rest at arresting tuberculosis infection. Domagk has had virtually no recognition for this discovery; when 5% of a continent's population is being slaughtered by war, there is no interest in cures for slow, wasting diseases such as tuberculosis. Indeed the Nazi regime considered it undesirable to seek drugs that saved life when the population was being asked for massive sacrifices. Domagk did eventually present his results, two years after the war had started and at a conference in Vienna. Only delegates from the Axis powers [Germany's allies in the war] and a few from friendly neutral countries attended, and no enthusiasm for his discovery was reported.

A Lost Prize

This indifference to Domagk may well have been directed at him personally. Just as Britain and France had declared war, Domagk received a letter from the convenor of the Nobel Committee for Physiology and Medicine. Domagk had been awarded the Nobel prize for 1939 in recognition of his discovery of the antibacterial properties of Prontosil. The Nazi administration had been discredited by the Nobel Committee that bestowed the Peace prize; German dissidents had been awarded the Peace Prize while languishing in concentration camps. Hitler decreed that it was un-German to accept a Nobel prize. Domagk was nervous about accepting this honour and requested permission. The Chancellor of the University of Munster thought that the Peace Prize should be regarded separately from the Science Prizes; after all, the committees were based in different countries. The Science Prizes were decided by committees in Sweden but the Peace Prize was decided upon by a committee in Norway as it was considered that the Swedes were too war-like to deliberate on such a prize. The German authorities remained silent, neither telling Domagk that he could collect the prize nor directing him to refuse it. In November 1939, Domagk was arrested by the Gestapo on no declared charge, though Domagk was always convinced that it was because of the prize. He was released a few days later. He then travelled by train to Berlin at the end of November to deliver a lecture. Domagk was arrested again and, at Gestapo headquarters, he was coerced to write to the Nobel Committee refusing the honour.

Penicillin and Luck

By Norman G. Heatley

Norman G. Heatley was a biochemist on the scientific team that Howard Florey assembled to investigate penicillin at Britain's Oxford University in the late 1930s. As he explains in this selection, he joined Florey's laboratory in 1936 and began work on penicillin in 1939. Heatley goes on to describe in detail how he solved the difficult problems of growing *Penicillium notatum* mold and harvesting penicillin from it with the limited supplies available in a nation at war. He used a variety of containers, including pie dishes and hospital bedpans. He claims that luck played a major role in his success, just as it did in Alexander Fleming's original discovery of penicillin in 1928, which he recalls here.

Heatley also recounts a key experiment in which the team tested penicillin on mice infected with streptococcus. The drug, he says, considerably prolonged the lives of the treated mice, compared to untreated animals, and completely cured one. Emboldened by this result, the group designed vessels to grow the mold on a larger scale and, Heatley writes, was fortunate enough to find a company that could manufacture them quickly. In 1941, he explains, the group was able to make the first human tests of penicillin on six severely ill patients. He says that the drug cured five of them of their infections.

[I n the late 1930s], when I was a student at Cambridge, England, I most days passed a building at the corner of Downing and Corn Exchange Streets on the walls of which was incised in large capitals Louis Pasteur's stern warning LE HASARD NE FAVORISE QUE CEUX QUI SONT PREPARES (Luck only favors those who are prepared). I took this to heart, and later was equally impressed by Paul Ehrlich's opinion that

Norman G. Heatley, "Penicillin and Luck," *Launching the Antibiotic Era: Personal Accounts of the Discovery and Use of the First Antibiotics*, edited by Carol L. Moberg and Zanvil A. Cohn. New York: The Rockefeller University Press, 1990. Copyright © 1990 by The Rockefeller University Press. All rights reserved. Reproduced by permission.

successful research required the four Gs: *geschick* (skill), *geduld* (patience), *geld* (money), and *glück* (luck). Unfortunately he did not explain how to acquire the last of these. It seems to me that luck—and I mean good luck, or serendipity—has played an interesting part in the early history of penicillin, and I would like to offer some examples.

But first I must declare and acknowledge my own enormous luck in finding myself in Howard Florey's laboratory at the Sir William Dunn School of Pathology, Oxford, in 1936; and from 1939 having the privilege of working personally with him and his colleagues on penicillin. Strangely, that was not my first contact with penicillin because in 1934 or 1935, while in F. Gowland Hopkins's Biochemical Laboratory, Cambridge, I attended a Tea Club lecture on selective enzyme inhibitors. In the discussion afterwards the lecturer was asked if any other selective inhibitors were known; the answer included ". . . and penicillin, a curious fungal product described by A. Fleming." My curiosity was aroused and I took some trouble to consult what is now Fleming's famous 1929 paper in *The British Journal of Experimental Pathology* and to make notes on it. So when Florey spoke to me for the first time about penicillin in 1939 I at least knew what he was talking about.

Fleming's Luck

To start at the beginning, [I have] a photograph of Fleming's famous plate, the essentials being a staphylococcal plate culture contaminated by a fungus from which something is diffusing which is clearly affecting the bacterial colonies; this something turned out to be penicillin. Most would agree that Fleming was very lucky to have this demonstration, set up and completed by Nature herself, displayed before him; but I would maintain that it was also fortunate that it was disclosed to *him*, since he was particularly well-equipped to detect and interpret its significance. An adept experimenter, usually with the simplest apparatus . . . he was also interested in the more bizarre aspects of bacteriology—witness his "paintings" on nutrient media inoculated with pigmented bacteria that developed on incubation. No doubt his acute powers of observation must have been reinforced by his previous discovery of lysozyme. Let us consider the actual scenario of his discovery of penicillin, with regard to the research of the late Ronald Hare, as described in his book *The Birth of Penicillin and the Disarming of Microbes.*

In the summer of 1928 Fleming goes on holiday, unaware that he has been chosen by the Fates to take the first steps in introducing the antibiotics to mankind. Having made a wise choice of their agent, the Fates also arranged that one of his plates, inoculated with staphylococci but not incubated, should be contaminated with a spore of *Penicillium notatum*, and that the weather during subsequent weeks should provide the sequence of rather narrow temperature ranges required to produce the penicillin effect. Fleming returns from his holiday and goes through the pile of used plates on his bench, looking at them and discarding them into the tray of disinfectant. The plates are many, and soon they are piled up, clear of the disinfectant. But what is this? Gracious Heavens, he has discarded *the* plate! All is not lost, for the Fates have a messenger on hand in the form of Fleming's colleague, D.M. Pryce. Pryce makes his entrance, they chat about staphylococci and, to make a point, Fleming picks up some of the discarded plates. The Fates hold their breath. Yes! He picks up *the* plate, looks at it, and says "That's funny . . ." How fortunate that trays rather than buckets were used for discarded cultures and that D.M. Pryce was on hand at the critical moment.

Now for a little wild speculation. Before Hare's work mentioned above, which was published in 1970, it was sometimes said that had Fleming not made his discovery, someone else would soon have done so "because the time was ripe." But taking Hare's work into consideration, the chances of another spontaneous display of the effect seen by Fleming would seem to be very low. The phenomenon is simple, and surely anyone with the most limited microbial expertise should have been able to recognize and interpret it (though against this assertion it must be said that even Fleming himself missed it the first time around). The effect could theoretically have been generated at any time after 1881, when Robert Koch introduced media solidified with agar. But the fact remains that it was nearly fifty years after that date that Fleming made his discovery, although many other examples of microbial antagonism had been described during that time. And now another sixty years have passed. Has the effect ever been reported again? Or perhaps observed, but not reported? Or dare one speculate that the chances of another spontaneous occurrence of the phenomenon are so slight that so far it may have been a "one-off" occurrence? And this in spite of the probability that since the early 1940s *Penicillium notatum* has become a much more common component of at least some laboratory environments.

Growing the Mold

Compared with the heroic displays of luck at the end of the 1920s, its contribution ten years later to the work at Oxford was very low key, and to some extent related to the fact that Britain was at war. Because of this, the availability of laboratory and other equipment was capricious. For example, at one period the ordinary empty soft drink bottle became a prized possession, since a bottle of squash [a type of soft drink] if one were lucky enough to find one in a shop, would only be sold in exchange for an empty one. Thus the fortuitous acquisition of a large number of identical strong glass bottles early in the war aroused curiosity and mild satisfaction at the time but later was seen to have been a stroke of major good fortune. They had a capacity of 4–5 liters, were stable, could be picked up and held by one hand, and could be adapted for a number of purposes. Solvent transfer became a key process in the extraction and purification of penicillin, but large separating funnels were virtually unobtainable; with a minor adaptation a bottle provided a rugged and more convenient substitute. . . .

Cultivation of the fungus was simple. Medium, to a depth of 1–2 centimeters, was sterilized in a container closed by a cotton plug. With full aseptic precautions it was inoculated with spores of *Penicillium notatum* and incubated at 24–26°C for about ten days. The medium, which by then had become bright yellow and contained penicillin, was harvested from under the fungal mat. Because of the long incubation period it followed that if the target was to set up and harvest, say, thirty vessels per day, then at least three hundred vessels would be required. All kinds of containers were pressed into service—flasks, bottles, trays, pie dishes, tins [cans], and hospital bedpans. There may be a resonance here since the bedpans can be likened to enormous Carrel flasks, a utensil invented, I believe, in The Rockefeller Institute [by Alexis Carrel]; they must have been very common during this period.

These assorted culture vessels were very uneconomical of incubator and autoclave space and of labor, but by the end of May 1940 enough penicillin was available for Florey to set up a mouse protection experiment. It was a good example of the kind of simple, well-planned experiment giving clear-cut results which appealed to Florey, and I would like to summarize it as follows: eight mice were each given an intraperitoneal [into the abdomen] injection of virulent streptococci. One hour later, two were given, subcutaneously [under the skin], a single dose of ten milligrams of a certain penicillin preparation. Two others were given five milligrams then and four further doses, each of five milligrams, at 3, 5, 7, and 11 hours after infection. The other four mice, the controls, received no penicillin. About 7 hours later the controls looked very sick and died between 13 and 17 hours after infection. All the treated mice looked relatively well. Those receiving the single dose survived for four and six days, while of those receiving the larger, divided dose one died after six days and the other remained well until killed some weeks later.

This was most encouraging and the next day, a Sunday, future plans were discussed. The mouse protection experiment would have to be repeated and extended with different pathogenic bacteria, and the chemistry, pharmacology, and antibacterial properties pursued ever more vigorously. But the greatest need was to try to step up production since the yield was pathetically low: 1–2 units per milliliter of culture fluid or, in terms of pure penicillin, not more than one milligram per liter. Even at this time Florey was aware that penicillin would have to be tested in human patients before its manufacture could be seriously considered, but as he pointed out, a man is three thousand times as big as a mouse.

In peacetime this would be the stage at which one would seek a commercial firm to grow the fungus on a pilot plant scale, but in wartime firms had full order books and it was understandable that they should have been reluctant to devote scarce resources to the possibly difficult production of a material which was only potentially valuable. The answer was to try to grow sufficient penicillin at the Dunn School, and one of the most urgent needs was for a supply of better culture vessels. A large chemical glassware manufacturing firm was approached. Yes, they could make the glass vessels to our specification, but the mold alone would cost about five hundred pounds and delivery time would be about six months. This was a blow; at best six months seemed a very long time, and delivery could easily have dragged on indefinitely. Someone then had the idea of a ceramic vessel, perhaps made by the slipcast process. In this process the object to be copied, a teapot, say, is embedded in a porous mold which can be taken apart and reassembled after removing the pattern—in this case the teapot. The cavity is then filled with a thick suspension of clay, known as slip. The porous mold sucks out water from the slip which is in contact with it and after a suitable time the liquid slip is poured out, leaving a layer of semi-solid slip lining the cavity in the form of the original teapot. After this has become firmer it is removed from the mold, dried, and fired. The process is relatively cheap, whether for many or a few copies.

The piece of luck I have been leading up to is that when the idea of a ceramic vessel was brought up Florey said, with excitement, that he knew a physician in The Potteries, J.P. Stock, to whom he would write immediately. Stock replied by telegram that the only firm likely to be able to help was James Macintyre & Co. Ltd. of Burslem. The next day I was sent to Burslem and was amazed to find that during the three or four days that they had had our sketches they had actually made—not fired, of course—three prototypes, one of which was almost exactly what was needed. Minor corrections were made with the help of a pocket knife and three sample vessels were promised eighteen days later, the apparent delay being due to the several days required for firing in the tunnel kiln. The sample vessels arrived punctually on time and a trial run showed that penicillin was produced satisfactorily in them. A firm order was placed and the first batch of 174 vessels was fetched on 23 December 1940. Half of them were washed and sterilized the next day, and on Christmas Day were seeded with spores of the fungus, about two months after first contacting Macintyre & Co. The number of days of *avoidable* delay during that period must have been very few, perhaps nil [none]. Each vessel held one liter of medium in a layer 1.7 centimeters deep, and they could be stacked vertically for autoclaving and inoculation, and horizontally for incubation; over seven hundred were made eventually. Without Florey's acquaintance with Stock, and Stock's introduction to Macintyre & Co., the search for a firm willing to make the ceramic vessels would almost certainly have been fruitless.

Early Tests in Humans

There had never been any indication that penicillin was toxic to mice, but when a human volunteer received one hundred milligrams of a preparation of which ten milligrams had had no visible effect on a mouse, she sustained a rigor [chill or bout of shivering]. The same happened with a different volunteer. Was the rigor due to one or more impurities, or was it due to the active principle? If the latter, its clinical value would have been partially or wholly vitiated [destroyed]. The question was quickly answered by Edward Abraham, who showed that chromatography on alumina would separate the pyrogen(s) [fever-causing agent(s)] from the penicillin, as well as providing a purer and more active preparation. By good luck penicillin itself is not pyrogenic.

With the new ceramic culture vessels coming on stream, penicillin became a little more freely available, and within a year of the first mouse protection experiment six gravely ill patients had been treated with penicillin at the Radcliffe Infirmary, Oxford, with Charles Fletcher of the Infirmary acting as a liaison officer with the Dunn School. The response was striking, so I will briefly mention just one of these six cases. The patient was a four-and-half-year old boy diagnosed as suffering from a staphylococcal-induced cavernous sinus thrombosis, a condition almost invariably fatal. He had not responded to sulfapyridine [a sulfa drug] and just before the beginning of penicillin treatment he appeared moribund [dying]. After nine days treatment he had almost recovered. . . . Unhappily he died from a ruptured mycotic aneurism [burst blood vessel] but an autopsy was permitted which confirmed the diagnosis and showed that the lesion [wound caused by the infection] was resolving [healing], with the generation of healthy granulation tissue. Gordon Stewart in his book *The Penicillin Group of Drugs* comments on these six cases with admirable conciseness:

> The results were convincing, each in a different way, and the absence of toxicity was almost as impressive as the rapid therapeutic effect. . . . In the present day, when a clinical trial is becoming an exercise in statistics and bureaucracy, there is irony in the reflection that the massive efforts which followed were based upon a few toxicity tests in rodents, and upon a clinical trial in six selected subjects, two of whom died. Had the toxicity tests been extended to guinea pigs, penicillin might have been rejected; had current regulations been in force, it would have been ineligible for submission.

I think Stewart is referring here to the British Committee on the Safety of Medicines, a much-respected body of distinguished experts which was established in the 1960s. Is it too whimsical to suggest that our greatest piece of luck might be the fact that this worthy body did not exist in 1941?

Selman A. Waksman Discovers Streptomycin

By Selman A. Waksman

Penicillin was far from the only antibiotic discovered in the mid–twentieth century. In 1943, Russian-born microbiologist Selman A. Waksman, working at Rutgers University in New Jersey, isolated another important antibiotic, streptomycin. Waksman describes his hunt for antibiotics, which he compares to a hunt for lions or tigers, in this selection from his autobiography, *My Life with the Microbes.* He explains how his extensive background in soil microbiology helped him in his quest, while began in 1939. He says he also built on the work of his former student René Dubos, who in that same year discovered an antibiotic called gramicidin, made by a soil microorganism. Waksman stresses that, unlike Alexander Fleming's finding of penicillin through a lucky accident, his own laboratory's discovery of streptomycin and other antibiotics was the result of hard, systematic work in isolating and testing compounds from thousands of cultures of soil microbes.

In 1939, I started on a new type of hunt, one of the most peculiar and exciting that man has ever undertaken—a hunt for microbes that have the capacity to yield a new kind of life-saving drug. How can expeditions for lions and tigers compare, in the nature of their preparation and results achieved, in the anxiety due to the many failures encountered and in the joy of the final accomplishments, with this new form of hunting? How can a mere desire to kill wild animals, whether they be birds or rabbits, crocodiles or behemoths, compare with the search for microbes which might yield chemical substances that have the capacity to combat such devastating human diseases and epidemics as tuberculosis and bubonic plague, intestinal infections and typhus fever, typhoid and brucellosis, leprosy and syphilis? The human mind can visualize a hunter trying to kill a dangerous leopard or a lion. But can it visualize the attempt of another type of hunter to domesticate unknown microbes hidden in the soil or in a manure pile, in order to combat the numerous infectious disease-producing germs that lurk to attack man and animals?

During past history, notably since the days of Louis Pasteur, the investigator has searched for causes of infectious diseases or epidemics and for agents responsible for processes of decomposition or fermentation. There have been naturalists and collectors before who have searched all the wide regions of the world for drug-yielding plants or for new varieties of plants or animals which could be domesticated by man for the improvement of his crops and his flocks. But this new type of search was something different. This was a combination of a microbial farm, a chemical laboratory, and a battery of experimental animals all used for the purpose of determining the effectiveness of a new type of drug produced by microbes.

The stakes were high, and the game seemed worth the chance. I was fully prepared to undertake such a study as a result of my intimate knowledge of fungi, actinomycetes, and bacteria, their occurrence in soil and their physiology. The methods that we worked out for the occurrence of the organisms in the soil and their activities could easily be modified to fit the new problems.

A Risky Quest

Numerous questions presented themselves, however. Did I possess sufficient laboratory and other facilities to do a proper job on this new and difficult problem? How could I, working in a small laboratory, which had previously been devoted primarily to soil microbiological problems, expect to uncover hidden secrets that would tend to influence medical science and medical practice? I had only limited chemical facilities to attack a problem that was not only microbiological but also to a considerable extent chemical in nature. This type of problem required extensive animal experimentation to answer the various questions of potential toxicity of new preparations that we were going to isolate and to determine their activity in the animal body as compared to their action in the test tube. Such investigations were bound to involve large-scale production of antibiotics, in order to obtain adequate quantities for chemical, animal, and finally clinical experimentation.

It took considerable courage, perhaps even more naïveness, to attempt a problem of this nature. Looking back to that period, I now realize that it was almost presumptuous on my part to undertake this type of investigation. I felt, however, that I was prepared to handle the various aspects that might arise in connection with the study of the microbes. Since a large part of my doctorate training was in biochemistry and chemistry, I knew at least the chemical approach to the problems in question. There were available at the [New Jersey Agricultural] Experiment Station two departments of animal and poultry husbandry, where I could no doubt obtain some help for animal testing. Moreover, my close relations with Merck & Co. [a large drug and chemical manufacturing firm] carried with it potential collaboration in the chemical isolation and purification of new compounds, their large-scale production, and the evaluation in animals of their chemotherapeutic potentialities.

Where Have All the Bacteria Gone?

During the many years of my digging in the soil and in the manure compost, of searching for unknown microbes, I had thought of the fate of all disease-producing germs, whether they be fungi or bacteria, protozoa or viruses, whether they attack the human or animal body, big plants or small. They all find, sooner or later, their way into the soil. This occurs either in the form of human or animal excreta or in the dead bodies of the deceased individuals. What becomes of all these germs? Since they tend to disappear rapidly in the soil, the question was whether this is because they are unable to live in the soil, or because they are destroyed by the other soil microbes. If the latter were the case, to what extent could such microbes be utilized for the purpose of producing chemical substances which would have a similar effect upon the pathogenic germs, in culture or even in the human or animal body?

These or similar ideas had been uppermost in the minds of

many investigators beginning with that of Louis Pasteur some three-quarters of a century earlier. When he saw that a group of sheep infected with the deadly anthrax failed to develop the disease simply because the culture of the anthrax organism was contaminated with a harmless bacterium, he prophesied that "the time may come when we may utilize harmless microbes for combating harmful ones."

These ideas were certainly in the mind of Dr. [Oswald] Avery of the Rockefeller Institute [in New York City] when he asked me in 1927 to recommend to him a young man trained in the study of soil microbes, so that an attempt could be made to isolate from the soil an organism capable of causing the destruction of the pneumonia-producing germ, the pneumococcus. I recommended René Dubos, who had just completed three years of training in my laboratory where he was engaged in the study of a strictly soil process, the decomposition of cellulose [a fibrous substance from plants] by bacteria. When put to the task, he at once visualized the significance of the problem before him. Within five years, he succeeded in isolating from the soil a bacillus that produced an enzyme system which had the capacity to dissolve the capsule of the pneumococcus germ, thus making it sensitive to destruction by the white blood corpuscles in the human body.

This was in 1932. The same year, I undertook, at the request of the National Research Council and the Tuberculosis Association, to direct a project on the fate of tuberculosis germs in the soil. I assigned this problem to one of my students, who, after three years, demonstrated, as had many before him, that this germ does not remain alive for very long in the soil or in water basins.

Complex Interactions

In the meantime, I undertook myself, together with some of my other students, a comprehensive study of the effects of one microbe upon another when both are living in close association. The contemplation of the nature and activities of the microbial population of the soil gave much food for thought concerning the tremendous potentialities that these activities offered for a better understanding of soil processes and possibly the effect of soil microbes upon disease-producing organisms. Who could have had a better opportunity to contemplate such potentialities? Having wrestled for more than two decades with the problem of complex microbiological life and the manifold activities of microorganisms in the soil, in the manure pile, in the sea, and in the peat bog, I fully recognized the fact that microbes do not live in watertight compartments in these habitats, that, unlike those that cause human and animal diseases or the fermentation of beer, wine, or vinegar, they do not live in pure culture. On the contrary, in the soil and in the manure pile, they live in complex mixtures. How do they thus affect the life and growth of one another?

These and other questions kept puzzling me, and, at the end of 1936, I presented some of these ideas in a series of papers, in which I tried to summarize the knowledge existing at that time concerning the effects of some microbes upon others. I tried to draw certain broad conclusions, largely applied, however, to soil problems. The time was not yet ripe for me to undertake in full earnest the study of disease-producing organisms and their relation to soil microbes, although I had another student undertake systematic studies of the changes in the soil population as a result of enrichment with specific bacteria. The opportune time came about two years later when Dubos succeeded, in 1939, in demonstrating that by systematic study of the soil microbes, it is relatively easy to isolate microbes which are able to kill disease-producing germs, grown in pure culture on a large scale, that such cultures will yield chemical substances which have the capacity to kill the deadly germs not only in the test tube but also in the animal body, and that such substances could be utilized as chemotherapeutic agents for the control of certain human and animal diseases.

The Time Was Ripe

One may argue that there was nothing new in that scientific contribution. Every step was already known, notably the enrichment of soil with disease-producing bacteria, the isolation from the soil of microbes effective against such bacteria, the cultivation of such microbes in the laboratory, the isolation from their cultures of chemical substances effective upon various pathogenic bacteria, and the final action of such substances on the pathogen introduced into the animal body. This is all true. But to obtain the desired results required an analytical mind, an original co-ordination of all the facts, and especially a new philosophy, which reasoned out and combined these steps into a successive and successful sequence.

One can further speculate on the fact that the particular substance isolated by Dubos, gramicidin, or tyrothricin, as it came to be known later, did not prove to be an ideal therapeutic agent, that neither in its effectiveness nor in the range of its activity against bacteria could it compare with penicillin or with streptomycin, which soon followed. But it was the beginning of an epoch, it pointed a way, it opened a new approach. Pyocyanase, discovered [in 1888], also a microbial product, also active on disease-producing bacteria, both in the test tube and in the animal body, no longer attracted serious attention, because of lack of appreciation of the fact that here was a new field of science that was to yield great discoveries for alleviation of human ills. Alexander Fleming, a keen observer, discovered and named penicillin [in 1928]; this, as well, had to wait its turn to find practical application, remaining all these years a mere laboratory curiosity, like many other microbial products isolated previously. Numerous other substances produced by bacteria and molds were known even prior to this work, substances that had the capacity to destroy deadly germs; they were being discovered almost every year, from mycophenolic acid in 1895 to gliotoxin in 1935, both formed by fungi. Certain products of bacteria, equally effective, also were known.

There was needed a synthesis or a co-ordination of all these ideas. This came in 1939. The time was now ripe. Certainly it was ripe for me, if not for many others. Here were not only new facts, but a new approach. In my many discussions of this and similar ideas with Dubos during 1938 and 1939, as he was working on this problem, I became fully convinced that all my prior knowledge of the fungi and actinomycetes, of their occurrence and activities, gave me just the tools required for this type of approach.

Exciting Days

Who can forget the excitement of those early days? It was like immersing oneself in a whirlpool of new ideas, new facts, new methods, new interpretations, and new applications. Each new experiment opened numerous vistas for others to follow. Each newly isolated compound pointed to many others, more effective, less toxic. It is hardly possible to tell this story in full detail. . . . Only a few of these events can be recorded here.

The staff that I assembled for this study in 1939 consisted, in addition to myself, of three graduate students, one of whom was Boyd Woodruff, one assistant, and three visiting investigators. We proceeded to compare various representative cultures among the bacteria, fungi, and actinomycetes for their ability to produce chemical substances that had a growth-inhibiting effect upon various bacteria, including disease-producing forms. We came first in contact with the pyocyaneus organism that produced two known substances *pyocyanase* and *pyocyanin*. Although these did not prove to be very desirable for disease control, they enabled us to develop satisfactory procedures for testing purposes and methods for the extraction and purification of the active substance.

Whether it was sheer luck or my previous familiarity with the group of microbes, the next culture that came immediately to our attention was an actinomyces. Although the particular culture was different from those already known to me, I was thoroughly familiar with the methods for its cultivation. We utilized the same procedures for the isolation and testing of the active substance as we had developed for pyocyanase. The new material was found to be a red pigment, soluble in organic solvents, and highly toxic to animals. We named it actinomycin. As a result of close collaboration with the chemists and pharmacologists at Merck & Co., we established its chemical nature and action in the animal body.

Finding Drugs "the Hard Way"

The problem I now outlined in 1940 involved a tremendous amount of detail work. Thousands of cultures of microbes were to be isolated from soils or from other natural materials. These microbes were to be grown on various media or substrates. They were to be tested for their ability to produce, under different conditions of cultivation, chemical substances which would have the capacity to inhibit the growth of various bacteria, pathogenic and nonpathogenic. The promising microbes were to be further purified, selected, and retested under different conditions, to obtain the maximum yield of the desirable compounds. These would be isolated from the cultures of the microbes by various chemical procedures, then further purified and concentrated. They were to be tested for their activity against bacteria and other microbes. Their toxicity to animals would be established. Their effect on disease-producing germs in the animal body would then be determined before their potential properties as therapeutic agents could be evaluated. Finally, arrangements would be made for testing the more promising agents clinically for their ability to control infectious diseases in the human body.

These many steps involved in the isolation of new chemical compounds that possessed therapeutic potentialities could hardly be appreciated by those outside the enchanted circle. Numerous disappointments were bound to result. One could hardly say that we were very lucky in the immediate isolation of promising substances. Following actinomycin, we succeeded in isolating streptothricin. This proved to be a much more promising compound, since it was not very toxic and possessed highly desirable antibacterial properties. Still it had certain limitations. We were on the way, however. All that we needed was to isolate compounds similar to streptothricin but somewhat less toxic. This led [in 1943] to the isolation of streptomycin, which proved to be a desirable agent for the treatment of many infections not previously subject to therapy. Later, we isolated other antibiotics, none of which has so far [in the mid-1950s] superseded streptomycin, although some, like neomycin, possess highly desirable chemotherapeutic properties and found an important place in the treatment of many infectious diseases.

In my public addresses, I was often asked whether streptomycin was isolated in our laboratory as a result of observing a contaminated bacterial plate (it is to be recalled that this was the case of penicillin, isolated by Sir Alexander Fleming from a green mold, which he observed as a contamination on a bacterial agar plate where the bacteria did not grow around the mold colony). My usual reply was as follows: "No, not quite! We went about it the hard way. We isolated freshly some ten thousand cultures of different microbes. These were tested for their activity against bacteria. Ten per cent of them were found to possess such potentiality, thus giving us a total of one thousand active cultures. The latter were now grown on various liquid media, to find those which had the capacity to liberate freely the substances possessing such activity; ten per cent were found to yield such substances. This gave us one hundred promising cultures. Since the active substances produced by these cultures were unknown and since they all required different chemical manipulations for isolation and purification, we finally succeeded in developing procedures for the isolation of ten per cent of them, thus giving us a total of ten new compounds. When these were tested for their therapeutic activity in animals, some were found to be too toxic, others were not very active in the body or did not possess the desirable kind of activity.

Only one of these proved to be a successful agent, streptomycin."

This, of course, is only a story, since by this time we must have isolated and tested some one hundred thousand cultures; still, it is close enough to the truth. Among the various microbes that my assistants, students, and I isolated and tested for their ability to produce antibiotics, the actinomycetes proved to be the most fruitful. They yielded in our hands, and later in the hands of other investigators in numerous university and industrial laboratories, some of the most interesting and most promising antibiotics, about ten of which have . . . found extensive application in human and animal therapy, and in the nutrition of various animals [by the mid-1950s].

CHAPTER 3

Antibiotics' Golden Age

Penicillin's First Miracles

By Edwin Kiester Jr.

In this selection, Edwin Kiester Jr. focuses on the first successful use of penicillin on a human in the United States. The patient was Anne Miller, wife of a Yale University administrator, who was deathly ill with an infection caused by streptococci in March 1942. Kiester's account includes quotes from Miller and other surviving participants in her drama.

In addition to telling Miller's story, Kiester pictures the time before antibiotics, when bacterial diseases were often fatal and few scientists believed that drugs able to safely kill bacteria inside the body would ever be discovered. He briefly describes the research of Alexander Fleming, Howard Florey, and others that led to the development of penicillin, including the drug's first tests on humans in Britain. He explains how the United States became involved in finding ways to mass-produce the new substance, but he stresses that only tiny amounts were available at the time Miller was treated. After recounting Miller's miraculous recovery, Kiester concludes by evaluating penicillin's effects on society, stating that it "ushered in the age of miracle drugs" and "vastly changed not only the practice of medicine but also human expectations and attitudes about health." Kiester has written numerous books and articles about health, including several books for parents on the development of babies.

She had been gravely ill for nearly a month when the package arrived. Anne Miller, now [in 1990] a vigorous 82-year-old grandmother, remembers only dimly the fight to save her life half a century ago. Drifting in and out of consciousness, half delirious, her fever spiking above 106 degrees, the young wife of a Yale University administrator heard little of the whispered, wor-

Edwin Kiester Jr., "A Curiosity Turned into the First Silver Bullet Against Death," *Smithsonian*, vol. 21, November 1990, pp. 173–87. Copyright © 1990 by the Smithsonian Institution National Association. Reproduced by permission of the author.

ried conferences at her bedside as a streptococcal infection raged through her body. In vain, doctors at New Haven Hospital had tried every weapon of 1940s medical science—sulfa drugs, blood transfusions, surgery—then watched helplessly as each effort failed and the young woman went steadily downhill.

[Then], on March 14, 1942, they were down to their last desperate resort. They had obtained a tiny amount of a new, unknown drug developed in England that had never been used on an American patient before. The result would be an epochal event, a triumph of English and American scientific skill, dedication and luck that would transform the face of world health. But Anne Miller, the central figure in the drama, was unaware of it. All she knew about the new drug was that it came in a brown bottle in a brown bag. She remembers having smelled the faint odor of mustard seconds after receiving the first injection. The drug had an unfamiliar name. It was called penicillin.

When Germs Ruled

[In 1990, almost] fifty years after the first wonder drug burst on the world, the details are still vivid in the memories of the now 70- and 80-year-olds who participated in those heady days. But even for them, it is difficult to hark back to an era when infections like Anne Miller's were a major threat to human health, and blood poisoning was the horror of every household. In the early 1940s, such "germs" as streptococci, staphylococci and pneumococci laid low rich and poor alike. Battle casualties succumbed more often to infection than to bullets. Bacterial illnesses were a leading cause of death. Every hospital had its isolation, or septic, ward where patients with contagious diseases or draining infections were shut up for weeks or months until the infection subsided—or won.

Yet conventional medical wisdom had held firmly for years that drugs given internally would never defeat infection—not, at least, without killing the patient. "The best minds," recalls Sir Edward Abraham, a penicillin pioneer, "believed that antibacterials would not work because they would he toxic to healthy tissue."

True, the German scientist Paul Ehrlich, after 605 failures, had finally formulated an arsenic compound named Salvarsan that specifically targeted the syphilis organism and overwhelmed it, albeit sometimes with damage to the patient. And in the mid-'30s Gerhard Domagk, another German scientist, had found that the red dye Prontosil would cure mice of certain streptococcal infections. His discovery led to the development of the sulfa drugs, which did kill certain germs, but which also had some serious side effects.

In 1928 Alexander Fleming, at St. Mary's Hospital in London—in a story that has now ascended into legend—had accidentally discovered that a mold which, he said, had blown in through his laboratory window, had killed bacteria in an open petri dish. Fleming identified the mold as *Penicillium notatum* and called the bacteria-killing substance that it produced "penicillin." His paper attracted little attention; even Fleming regarded the event mainly as a curiosity, to be demonstrated at medical meetings. The stuff was too unstable ever to be useful, he said. Other researchers saw the potential of Fleming's discovery but were defeated, too, by the chemical's instability. Then, just before World War II began, penicillin research was taken up, almost as an afterthought, at the Sir William Dunn School of Pathology at Oxford University.

Research in England

When Anne Miller lay dying in 1942, there was one man in the United States who had seen penicillin's miracles with his own eyes. Norman Heatley, [in 1990] a shy, spry 79, lives in the English village of Old Marston, a few miles from Oxford University. In the spring of 1942 he was working at Merck & Company in Rahway, New Jersey. He had joined the Dunn School in 1936 as part of a research team being assembled by Howard Florey, an Australian physiologist. Another recruit was biochemist Ernst Chain, a German refugee. Florey believed that many of the answers to medical questions lay in understanding the body's chemistry, and he hoped Chain could provide them.

The team would eventually win the Nobel Prize in Physiology or Medicine, but it won no honors for harmony; the real miracle may have been that their findings could have been achieved by such a fractious staff. Sir Edward Abraham, who arrived at the Dunn School in 1940, says, "By the time Chain left, I believe I was the only one on speaking terms with him." By all accounts, Chain was brilliant, abrasive, mercurial and dogmatic.

In 1939, the Dunn School was flat broke: checks were bouncing at the bank. Florey and Chain put their heads together to identify research projects that might bring funds. Before coming to

Oxford, Florey had studied lysozyme, an antibacterial enzyme produced within the body, which Fleming had also discovered: Chain, after a study of snake venoms, had reviewed other naturally occurring antibacterials and in the process came across Fleming's early report on penicillin. The two men then decided to ask the British Medical Research Council and the Rockefeller Foundation for money to study the field of microbial antagonists. Penicillin was to be one among many. The projects, according to the proposals, would be pure, basic research. The proposals included a few comments, however, suggesting that the research might have future therapeutic value.

A Life-Threatening Infection

On St. Valentine's Day 1942, Anne Miller was pregnant. But only her obstetrician and two other people knew—her mother and her husband, Ogden. She already had three sons, Ogden jr., 9; David, 6; and Dwight, 4. During the previous autumn, she had nursed Dwight through a bout of strep throat, a streptococcal infection. Anne, a nurse herself, had worn a mask and gown against contagion, just as she had been taught during her training. By St. Valentine's Day, the boy seemed to have fully recovered from his protracted illness.

Whether the boy's strep-related illness led to his mother's strep infection will never be known. But sometime after midnight she awoke and knew at once she was having a miscarriage. Ogden telephoned her obstetrician, and within minutes Norman Creadick was hurrying off to New Haven Hospital. A quick examination confirmed her fears. But the obstetrician knew immediately that hers was not an ordinary miscarriage. Her temperature was nearly 105, frighteningly high for an adult, and she was experiencing severe chills.

"Dr. Creadick told me, 'Don't even get dressed,'" Anne Miller recalls. "He called an ambulance and they just bundled me up, still in my wrapper [robe], and carried me down the stairs into the ambulance." She was rushed to the New Haven Hospital isolation ward, where a blood test showed that her bloodstream was riddled with bacteria. Creadick summoned her family physician, internist John Bumstead.

Dudley Miller, Anne's brother-in-law, was administrator of the hospital in 1942. "It was touch and go almost from the start,"

Miller, 87 [in 1990]: remembers. "Even at first, her blood count showed as high as 25 bacterial colonies per milliliter, a huge number. She was seriously, seriously ill. When you turned away from her bed for a minute, you didn't know if she'd be alive when you looked back."

The doctors tried sulfa drugs first. The infection and high fever persisted. On February 21 her fever soared beyond 106 and she was given a blood transfusion the next day. She developed inflammation of the blood vessels in her pelvis and thighs. The veins were tied off, and she received a second transfusion three days after the first, then another, two days later. The fever reached almost 107. The doctors tried scarlet fever serum, then rattlesnake serum, to no avail. The bacterial colonies in what should have been germ-free blood were counted at 25, 50, 100. It seemed obvious that, short of a miracle, 33-year-old Anne Miller was doomed to die.

First Tests of Penicillin

The miracle Anne Miller needed was not that far away, in Rahway, New Jersey, in the lands of Norman Heatley, who had recently come from the Oxford group to work on penicillin at Merck Laboratories—but that gets ahead of our story. Three years earlier, before the Oxford group received a $5,000-a-year grant from Rockefeller, Ernst Chain set out to analyze penicillin's bacteria-killing properties. Within a year he had drawn a chemical picture of the complicated compound and shown repeatedly that it could destroy certain types of bacteria in test tubes.

By then, World War II had broken out. "The professor [Florey] began to think of the implications for war wounds," Heatley says. "We knew that in World War I there had been enormous casualties from gas gangrene, for example, and our crude penicillin seemed to be effective against the gas gangrene organism. That stimulated us to work as hard as we could." Before long, basic research into antibacterials had been diverted into concentrated work on penicillin.

By early 1940, the experimenters had obtained enough penicillin to convince Florey to test it on infected animals. By the standards of today's laboratory protocols, penicillin's first live test was deceptively simple. Eight mice were given a potentially lethal injection of streptococci. About an hour later, two were given a single dose of penicillin, under the skin. Two others received multiple doses, spaced at two-hour intervals. The remaining four, the controls, were left untreated.

Heatley was assigned to stay with the animals throughout Saturday afternoon. After several hours, the untreated animals began to look ill. "Some friends of mine home from the RAF came by, and we went out to dinner," he recalls. "I stayed with them until about 10 P.M., then came back to the laboratory. The sick mice were looking considerably sicker, but the others were still healthy and frisking about. After about 13 hours, one mouse died. I stayed until about 3:45 A.M. All of the untreated mice were dead, but the others were still healthy. The results could not have been more clear-cut so I went home."

Testing on Humans

The very next morning, Heatley recalls, plans were drawn up to extend the test to humans. The first problem was to increase the yield of penicillin. Even the tiny amounts of the drug used for the mice represented at least an entire week's production.

Over the next year, the research laboratory was transformed into a penicillin factory. The mold seemed to grow best in very shallow containers with a large surface area of culture medium. Thus penicillin was cultivated in laboratory dishes, serving trays, pie plates, cookie tins, milk bottles on their sides—stacked everywhere, one atop another. Eventually the group found the ideal culture vessel—old-fashioned, covered bedpans borrowed from nearby Radcliffe Infirmary.

Florey decided to try penicillin on humans in early 1941. But first he had to prove its safety. He asked the Radcliffe Infirmary director to arrange a trial on a dying patient. Florey was describing his proposal when a young hospital physician, Charles Fletcher, entered the office.

Fletcher, who became a prominent respiratory specialist and [in 1990 was] in retirement in South London, remembers the meeting as if it were yesterday. "Florey explained that they had developed this remarkable stuff that seemed to have the extraordinary property of being able to kill strep infections in mice. There was no reason to suppose that it might be harmful to humans, but first they wanted to test it for toxicity on a patient with a fatal disease, someone who was going to die anyway. They wanted me to find such a person. I agreed immediately."

Success and Failure

A first trial, for toxicity, was compromised by impurities in the penicillin batch. Fletcher then chose a 43-year-old police constable, Albert Alexander, who had been scratched near the mouth by a rose thorn. The simple wound had developed both staphylococcal and streptococcal infections. Alexander had multiple abcesses of the head and face; his lungs were infected; one eye had been removed. He was in great pain and the only hope was for a merciful death. Fletcher developed an intravenous drip method, which would infuse penicillin at a slow, steady level, and began the treatment one afternoon. By next morning, Alexander's fever fell and he began to improve.

One of the characteristics of penicillin is that much of it passes unchanged through the body and is excreted in the urine. Half or more of a dose can be recovered. Florey quickly saw a method of extending the meager supply. Each day, Fletcher took the policeman's collected urine and bicycled across Oxford to the Dunn School, where the penicillin would be separated from the urine and returned for reuse. With each exchange, however, some penicillin was lost. By the fifth day, Alexander's fever disappeared; he sat up and ate; the infection appeared to be muted. But then the penicillin gave out. Alexander clung to life gamely for another month. But finally, after being on the brink of recovery, he died.

It was crushing to be so near success and then to fail. Yet it was also tremendously encouraging. As Fletcher says, "Nothing so remarkable had ever happened before." The team felt sure now that penicillin could defeat human infection—if they had enough of it. They decided to stretch the slim supply by treating only children, who required smaller amounts, or adults with localized infections. Fletcher's next candidate was a man with a carbuncle four inches in diameter—"Few doctors nowadays can have seen a carbuncle like this." Fletcher injected the carbuncle with penicillin and after five days it "had just melted away." He then tried penicillin on two children and an infant with serious infections, with excellent results in two of the three cases.

Another case ended tragically. Fletcher chose a 4½-year-old boy with a cavernous sinus thrombosis, an expanding blood clot within the skull, usually the result of an eye or nose infection. The condition, scarcely known to medicine today, was considered a sure death sentence. Sulfa drugs had been useless. The eyes of the feverish, delirious child were bulging pathetically and were completely closed by the condition; Fletcher gave him only a few hours to live. Fletcher administered the first dose of penicillin; the response was encouragingly rapid. The boy's fever dropped; his eyes returned to normal. Within a week, he was sitting up and playing with his toys. Then tragedy struck. A weakened blood vessel burst and he died within minutes. An autopsy showed that the condition had been cured, but that the blood vessels had been damaged by the thrombosis.

The six cases convinced Florey that penicillin was a proven commodity, ready for mass production. But the threat of a German invasion of Britain was considered so real that Florey had instructed each team member to smear some of the precious mold in his coat lining, so that the supply would be preserved "in case the panzer divisions roll down Headlington Hill," as Heatley recalls.

Penicillin Comes to America

America, with a burgeoning pharmaceutical industry, was Britain's unofficial ally and was well out of the range of Nazi bombs. Florey had U.S. connections through the Rockefeller Foundation. Moreover, an American friend was sheltering Florey's children for the duration of the war. He was the renowned neurophysiologist John F. Fulton, at Yale.

Neither penicillin nor the concept of antibiotics was wholly new to American scientists. In 1935, Roger Reed, a graduate student at Penn State, had stumbled across Fleming's discovery. He confirmed both its antibacterial effects and its instability. As a graduate student, however, he had no funds to pursue his research and was actively discouraged by his professor, who saw no future in penicillin. Reed's work stopped. Then, in 1939, the great René Dubos, at the Rockefeller Institute, discovered gramicidin, now said to be the first antibiotic. Isolated from soil, gramicidin halted bacterial growth and checked staphylococcus infections in mice. Unfortunately, just as other scientists had predicted, it also destroyed red blood cells and killed the mice.

In 1940, Martin Dawson and Gladys Hobby, at Presbyterian Hospital in New York, obtained some of Reed's penicillin, successfully treated some mice with it and then tried it on humans. Hobby, [by 1990] retired in Kennett Square, Pennsylvania, recalls that Dawson was driven by a desire to cure bacterial endocarditis, an inevitably fatal infection of the heart valves.

Dawson's first patients actually preceded those at Oxford and

Anne Miller, Hobby recalls. But none was cured. "We found later that we had given doses far too small to have had much effect," she says.

Seeking a Miracle Drug

None of this American history was known in New Haven in March 1942, where both Anne Miller's family and her doctors had all but abandoned hope. One entry on her hospital chart for that period shows the infinity symbol for the number of bacterial colonies in her blood.

John Bumstead, her family doctor, was at her bedside when he received news that another patient of his was in the isolation ward—Florey's friend Dr. John Fulton.

Fulton had been commissioned to study an outbreak of a respiratory illness in California military installations. In the process he had contracted the disease himself—a fungus-borne disorder called San Joaquin Valley fever—and had come home to be hospitalized. Bumstead, Fulton recorded later in his diary for March 12, came in, sat on his bed and related the sad plight of Anne Miller and the apparently futile struggle to save her life. By then, her fever had been peaking between 104 and 106.5 for 11 consecutive days. Bumstead asked Fulton to help him obtain Florey's remarkable "miracle drug."

Fulton called the Merck plant in New Jersey. Heatley was ready. "As soon as we received approval, we prepared the desired amount of penicillin and sent it off," he says. The exact method of delivery seems lost to history. Fulton's diary says the precious penicillin was sent by airmail. Heatley recalls dispatching a Merck messenger who, he believes, traveled by train. Dudley Miller tells an exciting story in which New Jersey state police sped the messenger to the state border, turned him over to New York state police, who in turn transferred him to a Connecticut state police escort. By whatever route, the package was delivered into eager hands at New Haven Hospital shortly after noon on Saturday, the 14th.

Return to Life

Now that they had the mysterious stuff, no one knew quite what to do with it. That is the recollection of Dr. Thomas Sappington, who was then an isolation ward intern. "We had no guidelines to follow," he says. "We didn't know the proper dose, nor how often it should be given, nor for what duration. We didn't have much, either—about five grams was all they could spare, about a teaspoonful. I had one clear instruction about penicillin. Don't drop it on the floor.

"After some discussion," he continues, "Dr. Bumstead settled on a test dosage of [850 units]. We dissolved about a gram of the drug in saline solution, passed it through a filter to remove any wayward bacteria and injected it about 3:30. When she seemed to tolerate it well, it was decided to give [3,400 units] every four hours through the night."

Bumstead administered the initial injection, with Sappington and other staff looking on. Later the task fell to Sappington, who recalls with a groan pulling himself out of bed at midnight and 4 A.M. Thus, the newly graduated physician, only a few months out of medical school, was the first to see Anne Miller come back to life. "Here was this attractive-looking young lady who was dying on Saturday," he recalls, still with a tone of awe, "and on Sunday her temperature was normal, she had come back to her senses, she was able to eat and all her vital signs were stable. Nothing in my whole experience has ever compared to that, nothing like it had ever happened before."

Fulton was equally excited. He wrote in his journal on Monday: "By 9 A.M. Sunday her temperature was normal for the first time in four weeks and has stayed normal until this writing. . . . She has eaten several enormous meals—also for the first time in four weeks. It really looks as though Florey had made a ten-strike of the first water, and I am glad we have had opportunity to make the first clinical trial of the American extract here."

By Sunday afternoon, Anne Miller was acting almost as if she had never been ill. She was able to sit up and greet her husband and inquire about the children. Dudley Miller remembers: "She was weak, she had lost considerable weight, but she was almost her old self again." Anne Miller's own recollections of the first few days are cloudy. "But I do remember that what I wanted most was to get out of bed, out of the ward, and breathe fresh air again."

A Health Revolution

By [late-twentieth-century] standards, Anne Miller received only small doses of penicillin; a million units per dose is commonplace

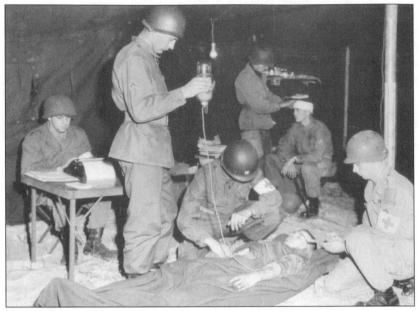

The use of penicillin to treat sick and wounded soldiers helped the Allies win the war. The success of the drug sparked an antibiotic revolution.

[in 1990] but the maximum she was given was calculated at 35,000 units—the precious supply was scant and had to be carefully doled out.

The miracle of Anne Miller elated not only her grateful friends in New Haven but the scientific world as well. "The hospital has been very excited because of the extraordinary results," Fulton recorded in his diary. At Merck, Heatley recalls, the news of Miller's amazing recovery—and Merck's role in it—galvanized the production process. Charles Pfizer & Company, another pharmaceutical firm, now agreed to begin making penicillin; before long, several other firms had joined in. The early supplies were designated for the military, but fortunately by November 1942, when a fire at the Coconut Grove nightclub in Boston claimed more than 500 lives, there was enough penicillin available to treat civilian burn victims.

The health revolution brought about by antibiotics was almost instantaneous. In 1943 Selman Waksman of Rutgers University [in New Brunswick, New Jersey,] announced the discovery of streptomycin, a new antibiotic effective against infections that penicillin could not reach. Before long, a whole armamentarium of antibiotics had been introduced and were in wide use.

Rocko Fasanella, a semiretired professor of ophthalmology [eye structure, function, and diseases] at Yale who was a medical student assisting at Anne Miller's bedside in 1942, has made himself an amateur historian of America's—and Yale's—contribution to penicillin. "American penicillin won the war," Fasanella says. "People talk about the impact of the atomic bomb. But I think the discovery of penicillin was equally important." German and Japanese scientists knew of Fleming's discovery, Fasanella points out, but were unable to follow up and put the drug into production. The Allies, on the other hand, had enough penicillin by D-Day, in 1944, to treat all serious British and American casualties of the European invasion; before the war ended, penicillin was already being released for civilian use. Even military personnel with certain venereal diseases were quickly cured and sent back to duty.

After the war, the antibiotic revolution vastly changed not only the practice of medicine but also human expectations and attitudes about health. Bacterial illnesses virtually disappeared as major causes of death, and isolation wards were eliminated. Life expectancy lengthened, focusing attention on the chronic diseases of longer life, such as diabetes, heart problems and cancer. As chemotherapy proved itself, the American pharmaceutical industry blossomed into a multibillion-dollar industry.

In 1945, Florey, Chain and Fleming received the Nobel Prize. Fleming, thanks to the appealing story of his accidental discovery, became an international celebrity, although he always insisted gallantly that others had been more responsible for penicillin's development. Florey's Oxford team continued their antibiotic research, which led to the discovery of cephalosporin and helped in the development of new varieties of penicillin that could combat "bugs" that were resistant to the original penicillin. Chain left Oxford bitterly, believing he had never received proper credit for his work and that the American drug industry had cashed in on his research.

With time, penicillin itself was seen as an incomplete miracle. It could not reach all infectious and created allergic, even fatal, reactions in susceptible persons. But it ushered in the age of miracle drugs and, with it, today's age of high-tech medicine.

"My Most Important Patient"

On May 8, 1942, Anne Miller left New Haven Hospital for the home she had never expected to see again. The first beneficiary of the era of wonder drugs had lost 40 pounds from her 5-foot-8, 130-pound frame and had grown her first gray hairs. The three months of hospitalization in those preinsurance days had "cost us a fortune," she recalls, which would not be paid off for several years. And she still did not feel totally healthy. "It was August before I was up to running a house again," she says, "and a year before I was my normal self. But I was alive, and back with my husband and boys."

In 1945 Ogden Miller left Yale to become headmaster of the Gunnery School, in Washington, Connecticut. He died in 1979 at age 78, but [in 1990] Anne Miller still lives in this picture-postcard New England town, surrounded by her memories and photographs of her six grandchildren. Despite the removal of a malformed kidney, and a few bouts of minor illnesses, she remains a picture of health—healthy enough to drive herself to Cape Cod for her annual summer vacation, to go to Texas for a grandson's wedding, to show a visitor around the Washington town green.

Three months after Anne Miller's recovery, Sir Alexander Fleming came to New Haven and sought her out. The picture of their meeting still occupies a place of honor in her home. "He was a small man, very courtly with big, soulful eyes," she recalls. "I shook his hand and thanked him for what he had done. He looked at me with those big eyes and said, 'Thank you, Mrs. Miller, you are my most important patient.'"

Anne Miller had never been Fleming's patient, of course, but when you have miraculously been given back your life, you are not one to quibble about details.

An Early Warning of Danger

By Carol L. Moberg

Carol L. Moberg states in this selection that as early as 1942, when the world was first becoming aware of penicillin as a "miracle drug," antibiotic pioneer René Dubos warned that bacteria would develop resistance to this or any other antibacterial drug. At the time, she says, scientists knew little about how genes worked and were not even sure that bacteria possessed these elements; Dubos instead based his predictions on observations of bacterial ecology and evolution. He had discovered an antibiotic called gramicidin in 1939 (it proved to be too toxic for humans to take internally) and had already seen bacteria become resistant to it. In subsequent decades, Moberg writes, Dubos further developed his understanding of resistance and increased his warnings that this phenomenon could make antibiotics worthless if the drugs were overused.

Moberg, a Rockefeller University (New York) scientist who has studied the development of antibiotics with particular emphasis on the work of Dubos, provides the scientific background of Dubos's conclusion, which lay in both his own earlier work and the observations of other scientists. Paul Ehrlich and Alexander Fleming, she states, had noted development of resistance to other drugs, and Howard Florey had reported resistance to penicillin. Nonetheless, claims Moberg, Dubos's warnings were at first lost in the euphoria created by antibiotics' early "miracle cures." By the mid-1950s, however, she reports that other scientists were beginning to pay attention. Moberg mentions that Dubos criticized not only overuse of antibiotics in treating sick humans but also use of antibiotics to prevent disease and increase growth in food animals, which some groups today believe is a major contributor to resistance.

Carol L. Moberg, "René Dubos, a Harbinger of Microbial Resistance to Antibiotics," *Perspectives in Biology and Medicine*, vol. 42, Summer 1999, p. 559. Copyright © 1999 by The Johns Hopkins University Press. Reproduced by permission.

To regard any form of life merely as slave or foe will one day be considered poor philosophy, for all living things constitute an integral part of the cosmic order.—René Dubos, 1901–1982.

As early as 1942, microbiologist René Dubos predicted that bacterial resistance to antibiotics should be expected:

> In the analysis of the mode of action of antibacterial agents, it may be profitable to keep in mind that susceptible bacterial species often give rise by "training" to variants endowed with great resistance to these agents. In some cases, drug resistance may be due to changes in metabolic behavior. . . . [or] may result from a change in cell permeability.

Prediction of Resistance

One rather startling aspect of this first warning of an impending crisis in medicine is how early it appeared in the antibiotic era. Two new antibacterial substances—penicillin and Dubos's own gramicidin—were just emerging from laboratory research. These antibiotics were in the first stages of clinical trials and not yet available for general use. The gold rush for other antibiotics had not even begun when Dubos also warned that searching for more was not enough. Instead, his plea was directed toward finding more accurate knowledge of "synthetic processes of the microbial cell" and thereby obtaining highly specific ways to control bacterial growth.

Another surprising aspect of this prediction is that it predates the science of molecular biology. In 1942, questions were still unanswered about whether bacteria had genes and whether DNA was the genetic material. While modern bacterial genetics has since developed much knowledge concerning molecular mechanisms of antibiotic resistance, Dubos based his prediction on 20 years of research experience with ecological facets of bacterial adaptations. His observations of the interplay between organisms and their environments, whether in soil, laboratory cultures, or animal tissues, formed his broad knowledge of natural variability, plasticity, and antagonisms among microbial populations. This work led him to systematically develop an antibiotic of his own in 1939. By the time he issued his prediction three years later, bacterial resistance to gramicidin had been found and confirmed by other researchers.

A further surprise [at the end of the twentieth century], is that Dubos's perspective was neither particularly original nor alarming to medical scientists of that era. In the half century before antibiotics, the number of clinically useful drugs was limited (vitamins, a few hormones including insulin, arsenicals, and sulfonamides), and sporadic reports of resistance were considered negligible. However, the rapidity and magnitude with which antibiotics were introduced after 1942 set the stage for a large-scale problem with fatal consequences. In this regard, Dubos was timely and prescient in expecting "great resistance."

This prediction was the first of many issued by Dubos over the following 40 years. Once he grasped that bacterial resistance should be expected, he set about to probe deeper and to anticipate consequences of this phenomenon. One result was that he continued to predict that antibiotics, along with the increasing array of chemical therapies, could treat and control acute cases, but they could never eliminate infectious diseases. Also, his continuing work led to ever-broadening views of bacteria, hosts, and environmental changes. Based on his experiences, Dubos envisioned what could be called medical microbial ecology, where alternative approaches to infectious diseases would work with rather than fight against bacteria.

Scientific Background of Dubos's Prediction

The roots of Dubos's first warning on antibiotic resistance were grounded in abundant research concerning bacterial responses to external factors. What he found was an extraordinary plasticity of bacteria to adapt themselves amidst the constant warfare in microbial milieus. He observed that some bacterial responses are reversible while others are transmitted to succeeding generations. Today's discussions of drug resistance and bacterial genetics focus on concepts of mutation, operon induction [the process by which a group of genes performing a particular function is "turned on"], and recombination. Yet during the 1920s and 1930s there was no knowledge of how these responses operated. Dubos, of course, had no inkling of bacterial genetics in 1942. In fact, in 1945, while his first book, *The Bacterial Cell*, was in page proof, he inserted an addendum by C.F. Robinow describing late 1944 evidence that several bacterial species possess a discrete nuclear body. In essence, Dubos began describing the dangers of resistance in terms of resiliency and adaptability.

Dubos began his research on the "soil as a whole," to learn which microbes decomposed cellulose under a variety of soil conditions. The impetus for this ecological approach was a 1924 article by soil microbiologist Sergei Winogradsky, an outspoken critic of the artificial culture methods used since [the time of Robert] Koch and [Louis] Pasteur to isolate pure bacterial forms. The soil, he wrote, is "un milieu vivant sature d'un masse grouillante d'etres microscopiques, d'une variete defiant toute imagination" ["a living environment saturated with a swarming mass of microscopic beings whose variety defies the imagination"] and must be studied under natural conditions. It is not the "qualites immanentes" [inherent qualities] of a microbe which determine its role, he continued, "mais que c'est la lutte des cellules avec toutes ces rigueurs qui est le principal rouage regulateur et repartiteur de l'activite microbienne" ["but rather, the struggle of the cells, with all its difficulties, is the principal regulator and distributor of microbial activity"].

Each organism in a "battle of the cells" acquires a degree of specialization and must be able to respond. It is precisely these responses, Dubos learned, that may be under-, over-, or unexpressed in pure laboratory cultures where there is no competition. The battles he observed in various soils went beyond chemical reactions to produce biological adaptations. He reported that the number and type of microbes involved in degrading cellulose are determined by physical and chemical characteristics of the soil. More important, however, he observed that chemicals produced as a result of decomposition vary with both microbes and soil conditions. The continual feedback he recorded between microbes and cellulose contributes to the soil and its fertility. By linking microbial responses to both destruction and creation, Dubos began to appreciate that bacterial antagonisms are orchestral.

Specialized Chemistry

In 1927, Oswald Avery at the Rockefeller Institute for Medical Research hired Dubos. Avery wanted this young Ph.D. to find a substance to destroy the capsule of type III pneumococcus that he believed was responsible for its virulence. While solving Avery's problem, Dubos demonstrated three further examples of plasticity in bacteria.

First, he found that abundant pneumococci could be obtained when they had no competition. Dubos discovered the only way to get large enough quantities of pneumococci to work with was to manipulate several environmental factors in the culture medium. By removing oxygen, monitoring the age of bacteria, and eliminating commercial peptones, he cleared away the competitors and opened the way for unimpeded bacterial growth.

Second, he found he could train bacteria to perform highly specialized tasks. To do this, Dubos established experimental bacterial antagonisms in the soil and controlled their competition. He fed pathogenic bacteria in several soil samples one source of food, the capsular polysaccharide of the pneumococcus. He knew most microbes were unaccustomed to such diets, so he counted on them to remain dormant or starve. But one bacterial strain in one soil sample thrived on this unnatural high carbohydrate diet. From it Dubos isolated the responsible "antibacterial" enzyme, or antibiotic, which cured infected animals by removing capsules from pathogenic pneumococci and rendering the naked bacteria easy prey for the host's phagocytes.

And third, he found bacteria contain "adaptive" enzymes (now called "inducible" enzymes) that allow them to display a wide repertoire of behavior. When Dubos tried to produce large quantities of his newly isolated SIII enzyme, he found unexpectedly that the enzyme appeared only as a response to a single source of food. In contrast with "constitutive enzymes" that are always produced by bacteria, its adaptive enzymes express a selective and reversible behavior. The experiment provided a striking example, defined in biochemical terms, of how bacteria make adaptive responses to changes in their environment. While this means bacteria can display morphologic, physiologic, and even pathologic properties that are latent or masked, many of these properties are expressed only as long as the specific environment persists. Dubos found that by varying an environment it was possible to control which bacterial potentialities were expressed or repressed under those conditions.

In 1939, Dubos again took advantage of bacterial antagonisms and the fact that bacteria always produce "antibiotics" to make his discovery of gramicidin. Ironically, he learned that antagonisms were also the source of a new problem, namely bacterial resistance. He quickly conveyed his alarm that this phenomenon related to problems of infection and disease. In his Harvey Lecture in March 1940, he stated, "the readiness with which microorganisms selectively change their enzymatic constitution in response to change in the environment may . . . be of importance in determining the pathology of infectious diseases."

Dubos further hypothesized that antibacterial substances may act differently in laboratory media than in animal tissues, and still differently in tissues with active disease than in those with only passive infection. Once he and several others began to investigate the mechanisms and clinical effects of gramicidin, Dubos immediately grasped the interesting dilemma that both antibiosis and antibiotic resistance resulted from bacterial antagonisms, yet neither could be explained by a single theory.

Resistance Begins to Appear

A history of resistance to chemotherapies shadows their progress in the 20th century. Even before 1942, some striking examples of bacterial resistance were known. When Paul Ehrlich coined the word chemotherapy, he referred to a direct, selective action of a drug on infecting microbes—for example, the arsenicals against the spirochetes of syphilis. However, in 1907, while testing such a selective action of the dye fuchsin to treat mice infected with the protozoan *Trypanosoma brucei*, he found the microbes became resistant to the drug. Initially the parasites seemed eliminated, but when they reappeared and the chemotherapy was repeated, they eventually ceased to respond. Ehrlich also observed that trypanosomes could be rendered resistant to the arsenicals. These examples led to his coining the term "drug fastness."

In 1922, seven years before discovering penicillin, Alexander Fleming observed bacterial resistance to lysozyme, a widely occurring natural antiseptic in the body. With V.D. Allison, Fleming created this resistance by repeatedly culturing *M. lysodeikticus* in the presence of partially lethal concentrations of lysozyme, selecting and then subculturing the survivors. In 1929, Fleming was trying to learn which microbes were sensitive to his crude penicillin preparation. He was struck by the complete insensitivity of Pfeiffer's bacillus (now *Hemophilus influenzae*). Accordingly, Fleming "hit on the idea of incorporating sterile penicillin in the culture medium" as a way to isolate the bacilli from the other microbes. In other words, he took advantage of penicillin as a selective bacteriological weed-killer to remove susceptible organisms and to harvest the freely growing Pfeiffer's bacilli. . . .

Resistance to Penicillin

The emergence of microbial resistance to penicillin followed a path similar to that of [resistance to] sulfonamides and gramicidin. In brief, the original report on penicillin by the Oxford University scientists in 1940 prepared the way for expecting resistance. [Edward P.] Abraham and [Ernst] Chain were the first to show certain bacteria produce an enzyme they named penicillinase that could potentially render bacteria resistant to penicillin. Their prediction has been realized to an extent no one thought possible, for penicillinase continues to be a critical aspect of bacterial resistance to the beta-lactamase antibiotics [those that attack bacteria with the enzyme that penicillin uses].

The next Oxford report gave details for producing, extracting, purifying, and testing penicillin. The researchers also demonstrated considerable differences in sensitivity to penicillin by different strains of the same organism. Included in this paper were details on the development of bacterial resistance to the drug. They were able to increase resistance in a strain of *Staphylococcus aureus* a thousandfold by subculturing the organism in increasing concentrations of penicillin over a nine-week period. However, contradicting the 1940 findings, they reported this staphylococcal resistance did not depend on the bacteria's ability to produce penicillinase. In 1949, the Oxford scientists concluded there was little correlation between the resistance conferred on an organism by its penicillinase production and its sensitivity to penicillin, and they suggested penicillinase resistance might be largely an artifact, important only when there were numerous cells and limited penicillin. From a contemporary viewpoint, this erroneous conclusion reveals they did not appreciate or anticipate the extent of horizontal genetic transfer inherent in the prokaryotic world. It is still unknown when and in what context beta-lactamase (penicillinase) first evolved—that is, in which bacteria and whether the first beta-lactamase was selected in the presence of penicillin produced "naturally" or by human pharmacology.

Resistance to penicillin among patients was also reported by the Oxford scientists. The first clinical trial of six patients during the spring of 1941 at Radcliffe Infirmary used a total of nearly 2 million units of penicillin, or one-half of Norman Heatley's 18-month production. Even then, one patient died when supplies ran out before curing his infection. Nonetheless, the small trial established penicillin as a powerful, safe cure for bacterial infections.

In 1943, during the second clinical trial of 15 patients, all but one recovered completely from infections that previously would have been considered hopeless. The one exception was a case of subacute bacterial endocarditis, in which the microbe *Streptococcus viridans* became resistant to penicillin and the patient died. The Floreys [Howard and Ethel] concluded their clinical report: "There are reasons for believing that organisms will sometimes develop resistance to penicillin during its administration. It has previously been shown that this can occur *in vitro*. Even on this ground alone, fully adequate dosage must be given at the beginning of treatment." Florey, like Fleming before him on sulfa drugs, concluded subeffective doses caused *in vivo* resistance, particularly among the many highly resistant strains of staphylococci. This opinion was reiterated by Florey and colleagues in their 1949 summary of resistance to penicillin:

> Certain organisms can become more resistant *in vivo* when infected animals are treated with subeffective doses, and there is some evidence that the same can happen to a limited extent in man, though not often. . . . The development of resistance *in vivo* is, however, relatively rare. . . . Fortunately, the staphylococcus is almost alone among the organisms for which penicillin is commonly used in having a substantial proportion of strains which are naturally highly resistant.

Unlike Dubos, these penicillin workers failed to relate microbial resistance to some broader issues of naturally changeable bacteria.

Dubos Renews His Warnings

There are several possible reasons why early warnings of bacterial resistance went unheeded. Articles focused on successful medical cures produced by the drugs, and incidents of resistance, when reported, were buried in medical scientific literature, read perhaps by only a few concerned laboratory scientists, and by even fewer physicians. The failures, lack of responses, or bacterial resistance thus were eclipsed by the overwhelming triumphs. Furthermore, when measured against genuine, even miraculous, cures from previously fatal infectious diseases, cases of resistance were statistically insignificant. Finally, to a majority of microbiologists of the time, the germ theory of disease was doctrine and meant disease could be eliminated simply by removing the responsible microbe. To these believers, antibiotics seemed a definitive answer to eradicating infectious diseases.

Fortunately, Dubos was not content with a single early warning. In 1944, before penicillin was available to civilians, he surveyed the state of infectious diseases for the American Philosophical Society. In the symposium "Wartime Advances in Medicine," he placed his original warning of resistance in a more ecological context. He argued that the new chemotherapeutic agents were only one facet of infection, reminding his audience that these drugs had no part in controlling smallpox, yellow fever, typhoid, or diphtheria. He urged study of the "natural history" of infectious disease along broader channels of virulence, immunity, and host response, all of which he noted are complex, vary independently of each other, and are focused on well-defined components of a pathogenic microbe.

In particular, he stressed that microbes "exhibit an extraordinary plasticity and can undergo profound variations of their biological properties." The medical significance of variability, he warned, is that

the development of drug-fastness has been recognized *in vivo*. . . . There exists the possibility, therefore, that [as] a result of the widespread use of sulfonamides in therapy and especially for prophylaxis, there may develop in the population strains of pathogenic agents which have become resistant to these drugs. . . . Although there is as yet no evidence of any real danger, the problem should not be ignored, and it is to be hoped that laboratories throughout the land will find it possible to maintain a permanent survey in order to follow the shift in susceptibility of the different pathogenic agents to the drugs in common use.

The following year, in 1945, Dubos elaborated on this warning in his monograph *The Bacterial Cell*. He provided ample experimental evidence from others that resistance could be obtained and explained by more than one mechanism. Among these mechanisms, drugs compete with an essential metabolite and cause a condition similar to nutritional deficiency; drugs can alter any number of properties of the bacterial cell, such as decreasing permeability that prevents or retards a drug from reaching its susceptible structure. He stressed the complexity of infection and the various attributes that produce resistance:

Since so many of the properties and characters of bacteria can undergo independent variation . . . drug fastness can occur without any alteration of virulence or can be associated with structural or metabolic variations which affect one or several of the factors of virulence. . . . It is possible, therefore that the widespread use of chemotherapeutic agents will favor the production of many unsuspected variants, exhibiting all degrees of drug fastness and of pathogenicity. . . .

A Worsening Problem

The first general awareness that something of real magnitude and clinical significance was amiss in antibiotic therapy came during the mid-1950s. Widespread use of antimicrobial drugs was displaying unexpected and varied effects. Of highest priority were problems of resistant strains of staphylococci in the hospital setting.

[In 1956,] fourteen years after his initial warning, Dubos was asked to summarize a conference devoted to staphylococcal problems. Physicians and scientists considered two problems: epidemics of staphylococcal infections in the hospital, and chemotherapies that facilitated both more virulent infections and resistance to antibiotics. Dubos chose to address the unknowns of the bacterial problem. He raised new issues of concern regarding the escalating antimicrobial resistance.

Dubos acknowledged staphylococci readily undergo genotypic or phenotypic changes that make pathogenicity difficult to characterize. But he offered another way to consider the problem. Whatever the origin of the variant, he said, the "organisms that initiate the disease may become profoundly altered in . . . an abscess [and] may have lost temporarily some of the very properties that had first endowed it with invasive power." The biochemical site of infection determines whether vaccines establish acquired immunity and whether antibiotics control microbes.

To study this problem, he urged research on strains of bacteria as they occur in diseased tissues rather than in laboratory subcultures. Besides identifying serological types and drug resistance, he insisted on identifying components and substances produced by bacteria in their microenvironments during pathogenesis. The goal, he explained, is to determine which local elements protect a particular bacterial strain from host defenses and drugs. Much like tubercle bacilli, he suggested, the staphylococci persist (in a masked state, a resting form, or sequestered in tissues) in humans or animals receiving chemotherapy, and these persisters "remain fully susceptible to the drug in use." In what form are the persisters, he asked, suggesting their metabolic state or life cycle contributes to stamina and/or resistance? What elements in the tissue environment, he queried, upset the equilibrium and change it from silent infection to active disease? And, what is the immune state of the host who is fighting this infection?

Dubos brought some of his ongoing research on staphylococci to bear on these points. With Russell Schaedler and Ian Maclean Smith, Dubos was studying the effect of nonspecific factors on susceptibility to infection in mice. Some nonspecific factors he tested in tuberculosis and staphylococcal infections were nutrition, starvation, uncontrolled diabetes, a variety of toxemias [forms of blood poisoning] and subclinical allergic reactions. Dubos's team was able to demonstrate that susceptibility could be increased, decreased, or, quite impressively, reversed. The determining factor in the outcome of infection, he observed, was the physiological state of the host and its local tissue environment. The outcome produced not only quantitative metabolic effects on staphylococci but qualitatively changed "the very characteristics" of the microbes themselves.

In the same year that Dubos addressed these problems of staphylococcal infection, [Howard] Florey told a group of Canadian physicians that "hospitals are bacteriologically dirty places":

> There can be little doubt that the prevalence of bacteria resistant to antibiotics is due primarily to the fact that surgeons, nursing staff, and practically every one who attends the patients, may be carriers of these organisms. . . . It now becomes very clear that we must tighten up the precautions against cross-infection.

Florey's solution was to apply stringent hygienic measures to prevent spreading an infection from one patient to another. He also urged the development of more antibiotics, this time drugs having a broader striking power. He strongly advised that such new antibiotics would demand wise and careful control.

In contrast to Florey and many others who advocated broad-spectrum antibiotics to fight resistant strains, Dubos condemned such "gun-shot treatments" [sic]. Speaking before an international conference on "The Use of Antibiotics in Agriculture," he predicted

broad-spectrum antibiotics would create new diseases while potentially curing ones for which they were intended. "Chemotherapy," he said of the broad-spectrum antibiotics, "can become the
cause of man-made diseases by permitting the multiplication of
certain microbial agents which cannot compete" with normal microbial flora in the tissues. He warned of dangers from feeding antibiotics to farm animals to increase food utilization and growth,
especially when these animals are kept in unsanitary conditions or
given deficient diets. Antibiotics that are used not to fight disease
but instead as prophylactics or as "growth factors" would allow
bacterial resistance and new diseases to breed unabated. He noted
that when entire aggregates of microbes are selected for elimina-
tion, because they are toxic or compete with dietary nutrients, this
vacuum creates a profoundly disturbed equilibrium between host
and microbes. As Dubos predicted would happen, the too-efficient
curb on microbes from using antibiotics has spawned some disas-
trous secondary effects on both animal and human populations.

The Antibiotic Revolution

By Gladys L. Hobby

In this selection, Gladys L. Hobby, a microbiologist who helped to prepare penicillin for mass production in the United States, describes the many ways in which penicillin and the other antibiotics that followed it in the late 1940s and 1950s changed medicine. First, Hobby says, the process by which penicillin was developed into a widely available drug provided a model of cooperation among government, industry, and academia. Even more important, she believes, the success of antibiotics both made infectious disease seem conquerable and made physicians and the public more willing to accept new drugs or treatments of all kinds. She claims that antibiotics also indirectly made possible such advances as heart surgery and organ transplantation.

Hobby points out that, in spite of their seemingly miraculous triumphs, antibiotics are not perfect. They do not affect all types of microorganisms (they are ineffective against viruses, for example), and they often cannot eliminate all disease-causing bacteria from the body, even when they prevent the development of disease. Once-susceptible bacteria, furthermore, can become resistant to them, she notes. She therefore feels that the belief that further research on infectious disease is unnecessary, which developed in the 1960s and 1970s because of antibiotics' successes, represents an overconfidence that is very unwise.

P enicillin was the first antibiotic developed to a stage allowing its controlled trial as a therapeutic agent for parenteral [injected] treatment of infections in humans. In 1940 it was, and it still is [in 1980], the most active antimicrobial agent ever described.

No one questions the impact that penicillin has had on science and medicine. Yet it is sobering to note that penicillin might not exist today if 1980 to 1983 concepts of ethical practices and 1980 to 1983 rules and regulations governing studies of new agents in human beings had prevailed in 1940 to 1942. Early preparations of penicillin were impure and highly pigmented; they contained pyrogenic [fever-causing] materials that would not be allowed in any pharmaceutical product today. Yet this crude material produced in people such dramatic therapeutic responses that the expenditure of massive amounts of human time and talent, precious supplies and monies, seemed justified.

Streptomycin, the second widely used antimicrobial drug, was discovered [in 1943,] four years after the Oxford group of investigators had first reported the isolation of penicillin in a crude but usable form. Streptomycin was active against a different spectrum of infecting organisms, and it was less active on a weight basis, more toxic, and more prone to allow the emergence of drug-resistant organisms than was penicillin. Yet it quickly became an accepted chemotherapeutic drug for treatment of those infections caused by microorganisms susceptible to its action. Knowledge of all that penicillin could do made it easy to believe that another antimicrobial drug could do likewise. Experience with penicillin had provided the base necessary for the development of streptomycin and, later, polymyxins, neomycins, chloramphenicol, tetracyclines, and the many other antimicrobials that followed.

Early interest in penicillin derived from the medical profession's need for a means of treating infectious diseases. Unquestionably, World War II stimulated and speeded its development. But even without such a stimulus, penicillin—or another agent—would soon have been introduced for treatment of infection. It would have taken longer for it to gain acceptance: penicillin might not have been first but the need existed. Interest in bacterial antagonisms and knowledge of the phenomenon of antibiosis were pointing the way.

Need for Talent and Cooperation

Dr. Vannevar Bush, director of World War II's Office of Scientific Research and Development, was asked by President Franklin D. Roosevelt in November 1944 to advise on how to organize a program for continuing the work that had been done in medicine and the related sciences during the war. Roosevelt requested specifically an effective program for discovering and developing talent in American youth so that scientific research in the United States would continue to function on a level comparable to that of World War II. Bush based his report primarily on the natural sciences, and the program he presented to President Harry Truman (who by then had succeeded Roosevelt) laid the foundation for much that transpired in the United States in subsequent years. The development of penicillin figured strongly in Bush's thinking and in his proposals; the establishment of the National Science Foundation was a direct outgrowth of this report.

Penicillin was developed at a time when investigators in industry, universities, and government were working closely together and the distinctions between applied and basic research were beginning to blur. Relations between universities and industry peaked as research on penicillin began to peak. Clinicians, biologists, and chemists at the university level needed the talent, the equipment, and the production know-how that industry could provide. They needed the impetus and dollars that government could provide as well as the scientific expertise available through government facilities and personnel. Thus, the development of penicillin became a prime example of what collaboration among government, industry, and the universities could achieve.

A Revolution in Medicine

The antimicrobial drugs available for clinical use in 1941 were quinine, quinacrine [a synthetic form of quinine], the arsenicals, and the sulfonamides. Only the sulfonamides were active against bacterial infections, and even these had a narrow range of utility because of their toxicity. By 1945, penicillin was in widespread use, and by 1960, seven classes of antimicrobial drugs had been identified: the beta-lactam antibiotics (including the penicillins and cephalosporins), aminoglycosides (including streptomycin, among other drugs), macrolides, ansamycines, polypeptide and depsipeptide antibiotics, and a few miscellaneous agents that did not fall into any of these categories. Together, these drugs brought about major changes in the incidence, mortality, and epidemiology of infectious diseases worldwide. By 1960, the world had seen a remarkable increase in the capacity of medicine to alter the course of many infectious diseases.

In 1982 Dr. Walsh McDermott attempted to convey his recollections of infectious diseases in the "before and after" penicillin period and called attention to the fact that few physicians now in practice can recall these diseases as they were in the 1930s and before. According to McDermott—and this was certainly true— it became clear almost immediately after penicillin was available for clinical use that lives could be saved by the proper administration of the drug. But time was required to establish changes in epidemiology and in those disease characteristics that influenced responses to chemotherapy:

> The bringing of each disease under control was in itself a separate miracle. These were thrilling events. If traditionally the medical profession was slow to embrace the new, it soon lost all such shyness. Therapeutic triumphs coming rapidly one after another imprinted the physicians with almost too great a readiness to believe. Faced with the tale of some new remedy, an impulse to seek proof would arise from the science-based portion of their education, only to be met by the internal rejoinder, "why not believe?" And, among the most poignant and enduring recollections would be those of the distressing terminal illness of the last patient on "the old" treatment, as contrasted with the "recovery" of the first patient on the "new" treatment . . . [gradually there] were changes in the ways . . . doctors practiced medicine and the extension of . . . things possible. . . . The impact of [antimicrobial] technology, and it has been great, has been on the extent to which by providing a potential control for infection it has expanded what . . . [physicians] can do.

The use of penicillin and the antimicrobial drugs that followed affected virtually all aspects of medicine. Not only did it decrease the incidence and severity of many infectious diseases, but, as McDermott reminded us, it made possible cardiac surgery, organ transplantation, and the management of severe burns. It decreased mortality due to hemolytic [blood-destroying] streptococcal infections, such as puerperal sepsis [severe infection following childbirth] and it changed the frequency and nature of infectious diseases seen in the practice of pediatrics. It also decreased mortality due to illnesses such as pneumococcal pneumonia, otitis media, and bacterial meningitis (though pneumococci, for example, remain prevalent [in the early 1980s] and are a major cause of community-acquired bacterial pneumonia—the incidence of which approximates one-half million cases annually in the United States—and otitis media in infancy and early childhood—the incidence of which exceeds one million cases yearly).

Persistence and Resistance

Pneumococci are among the organisms most susceptible to the action of penicillin. Yet they often persist for long periods of time following apparently adequate chemotherapy of infected hosts. Despite the remarkable antibacterial activity of penicillin, eradication of penicillin-susceptible organisms from infected persons occurs rarely, if ever. Microbial persistence, although difficult to detect, occurs frequently. The survival of drug-susceptible microorganisms within the host despite the presence of high concentrations of drug is a phenomenon that, once described, provided a basis for understanding the mechanisms by which late relapse may occur in humans.

As long as an infectious agent, whether a pneumococcus or streptococcus, a tubercle bacillus or other living organism, exists within an individual, that individual is infected. One cannot prevent infection, nor, at least from the microbiologist's viewpoint, can one easily eradicate infection. One can hope only to prevent the development of disease in the infected host.

The development of resistance of bacteria to commonly used antibiotics is one of the most important factors limiting the effectiveness of antimicrobial therapy [in the early 1980s]. Organisms resistant to the sulfonamides and to penicillin were described promptly after their first use in clinical medicine. Yet many organisms such as the pneumococci, hemolytic streptococci, and gonococci remained adequately susceptible to benzyl penicillin for many years. The introduction of a antimicrobial drugs initially active against some other organisms, particularly the *Enterobacteriaceae*, however, brought with it other problems. The spread of R-factors (resistance factors) among the *Enterobacteriaceae* and of resistance plasmids into unrelated bacterial species was the cause of deep concern.

Penicillin resistance, however, occurs differently. It relates to the capacity of an infecting organism to produce an enzyme, penicillinase (beta-lactamase), which destroys penicillin's antimicrobial effectiveness. This obviously limited penicillin's usefulness over the years. Penicillinase-inhibiting adjuvants [substances added to drugs to increase their effectiveness] as a class, however, are having a great impact on the treatment of infections caused by beta-lactamase-producing organisms [in the 1980s]. In mixed infections, moreover, where penicillinase-producing nonpathogens may protect pathogenic organisms from penicillinase-susceptible (unstable) drugs, the use of an antibacterial drug in combination with an inhibitor of the enzyme that destroys it offers promise.

The Danger of Overconfidence

During the 1960s and 1970s, interest in infectious diseases waned to some extent. Surely this is true of those diseases caused by antibiotic-susceptible microorganisms. It is difficult to retain interest in illnesses that do not occur or are easily treated even though historically they may have been most important at one time. It is difficult to retain interest in diseases one does not see, does not hear about, or in new and pathogenic microorganisms isolates of which one cannot obtain for study. But infection has not vanished and the prevalence of infectious diseases as a class has not waned. In 1980, there were at least two hundred known infectious diseases that could neither be treated nor prevented. Most were caused by viruses which mutate so easily that the development of specific and effective agents for their control has been difficult. Some are due to disease-producing agents that have long been known; some appear to be due to previously undescribed agents of disease.

Ironically, penicillin and the antibiotics that followed are responsible for the current lack of interest in infectious diseases. This indifference is a measure of the success of antibiotics in the treatment and control of infection. Yet, lest we relax too much, we must remember the remarkable capacity of microorganisms to persist, to mutate, and thus to thwart the efforts of the best of us.

CHAPTER 4

Antibiotics Today: The Threat of Resistance

Misuse of Antibiotics Contributes to Resistance

By Dr. Debra Fulghum Bruce

One reason that many bacteria are becoming dangerously resistant to antibiotics, explains Dr. Debra Fulghum Bruce, an Atlanta freelance writer whose specialty is health subjects, is that people take them inappropriately. They ask doctors to prescribe the drugs for infections that do not respond to antibiotics, for instance, or they pass leftover antibiotics on to other members of their families rather than throwing them away. Dr. Bruce stresses that antibiotics should be used only when needed and should be taken according to directions. Better still, she says, people can avoid using the drugs by keeping themselves and their families healthy. Measures she recommends include immunizations, disinfection of objects in the home, a diet that includes fresh fruits and vegetables, and a lifestyle that strengthens the immune system.

When Meredith started getting symptoms of a sinus infection [in 2001], this 44-year-old teacher and busy mother of three opted to call her doctor's office and describe the symptoms to the nurse instead of going in for an evaluation. After speaking with the doctor, the nurse called in a prescription for antibiotics to the local pharmacy. A few months later when Meredith was preparing for a family's vacation, she again called the nurse and asked for several refills of the antibiotic "in case she became ill."

Meredith did become ill and stayed on the antibiotics for four weeks, yet her dry cough and discolored mucus seemed to worsen. She also had a low-grade fever and body aches, and was extremely fatigued upon little exertion. Her pulse was fast, and she had lost weight. Meredith's husband convinced her to see her doctor, who diagnosed her with pneumonia and immediately admitted her to the hospital. Meredith was in the hospital on IV antibiotics (two different ones) for more than three weeks before the pneumonia was resolved.

[In 2002], while Meredith no longer harbors the bacterial infection, she is very susceptible to a relapse. Her immune system is still weak, forcing her to take a leave from teaching—all because of antibiotic misuse and bacteria that was resistant to treatment.

While it may seem puzzling that antibiotics could actually increase your risk of a life-threatening illness, as it did with Meredith, the problem of antibiotic resistance is becoming increasingly commonplace and threatens the lives of millions around the world. Consider that in 1941, 40,000 units of penicillin a day would cure a patient with pneumonia in just four days. Today that person may receive 24 million units of penicillin a day and still die. And even with the strongest antibiotics available, infectious diseases are a leading cause of death worldwide and the third leading overall cause of death in the United States.

The Alarming Resistance Process

It's easy to become confused about antibacterial resistance. And while many people believe that the body becomes resistant to the specific antibiotic, this is not true. It is the germs that become resistant to the drug, making it difficult—if not impossible—to treat the illness and end the bacterial infection. This type of resistance can occur in any type of germ, and exactly how germs become resistant is an incredible process.

According to the Centers for Disease Control, antibiotic resistance happens when microbes develop ways to survive the use of medicines meant to kill or weaken them. If a microbe is resistant to many drugs, treating the infections it causes can become difficult or even impossible. For instance, strains of resistant staph infections, which have become prevalent in hospitals, are now appearing in nonhospital settings, and several strains of this bacteria are becoming resistant to vancomycin, one of the most powerful antibiotics in our modern medical arsenal. Added to this is the fact that routine illnesses such as strep throat, cystitis, sinusitis, bronchitis, and ear infections are becoming much more persistent and difficult to treat.

Germs become resistant to antibiotic medications for different reasons. Sometimes this happens when you take antibiotics too frequently or take them for other illnesses for which they are not indicated. Then when you get a resistant infection, you can pass that same infection on to another person. In this manner, an illness that is resistant to antibiotic treatment can spread from person to person until you have an epidemic that can lead to serious illness, disability, or even deaths. Although resistant germs are prevalent everywhere, they have a higher incidence in places where people have close contact—hospital rooms for the chronically ill, nursing homes, crowded day-care centers, compact military quarters, and even on the streets among the homeless.

Making Peace with Germs

While germs are all over the place—in your body, on your body, and on everything around you—most assist in shielding you from infection as they restrain the duplication of pathogenic bacteria, those antagonistic microorganisms that make you ill and tear down your body's tissues. When you do get a bacterial infection, there's no doubt that antibiotics are miracle drugs. But where do you draw the line? While antibiotics can treat bacterial infections, many times they are used inappropriately simply because a patient demands the medication. Sometimes a doctor may "guess" which type of antibiotic to give without culturing the germ to find out the exact drug that can kill it. And when you consider that more than 12 million antibiotic prescriptions given to adults in the United States in 1992 were for upper respiratory tract infections and bronchitis—on which these drugs have little or no effect—you have to be alarmed!

Protecting Your Family

As with any threat to your health or well-being, knowledge is part of the solution when it comes to antibiotic resistance. There are also self-help strategies you can take to protect yourself and your family:

1. First, talk openly and knowledgeably with your doctor about antibiotic resistance, and do not demand antibiotics if you are ill. Your doctor will try to determine if you have a bacterial infection or a virus and should prescribe antibiotics only if necessary.

2. When your doctor prescribes antibiotics, use them exactly as prescribed. Finish all of the prescription, as instructed, even if you are improved in a few days. Do not save leftover pills "just in case" you or a family member might get sick later on.

3. Discard any remaining pills in a way so that others (particularly children) cannot get access to them. And do not give your antibiotics to anyone else. Likewise, do not take someone else's medication.

Staying Well

Along with knowing when to take—or not to take—antibiotics, it's vital to build your body's natural defense against infection. When our immune system falters, we battle the resulting lifestyle ailments, such as frequent viral infections, sore throats, colds, skin problems, and allergies, as well as bacterial infections. Yet if you can focus on changing lifestyle habits, including using self-care to treat an illness early on, your prevention measures may help to keep you well so you can avoid antibiotics altogether. Try the following stay-well strategies:

Get immunized. Because epidemics of influenza are responsible for an average of approximately 20,000 deaths per year in the United States, ask your doctor about an annual flu vaccination. While the flu is a viral infection (meaning antibiotics cannot cure it), you can get a secondary infection, such as pneumonia, or it can worsen chronic health problems, such as heart or lung disease. While the flu shot is no guarantee against the flu, it can help to lessen the symptoms if you do get it. Also, ask your doctor about the pneumovac (pneumococcal vaccine) to see if this may reduce your chances of getting pneumonia. Make sure you and your family are all current on the recommended immunizations.

Know if you are at higher risk for infection. While a cold virus may leave most of us feeling bad for a week, we usually get well without treatment. Yet there are some people who are at higher risk of infection and should talk to the doctor at the start of any illness.

Also, if you care for a high-risk person, such as an elderly parent or newborn baby, or work with people who are at high-risk for infection, take greater precautions to stay well, including getting the influenza shot each year.

Disinfection and Diet

Keep your house disinfected. Many preventable germs are harboring in your kitchen sink, your bathroom (particularly on the toilet seat and faucet handles), doorknobs, the computer keyboard, and the family telephone. While you don't want to become obsessed with cleaning, make sure that you disinfect your kitchen and bathrooms frequently. A disinfectant is a chemical used to destroy germs, and a homemade solution of household bleach and water is one of the most effective disinfectants. The recommended strength is one tablespoon of bleach in one quart of water, or mix one-fourth cup of bleach in one gallon of water. (After applying, let it air-dry or use disposable paper towels to wipe.)

As well as using this solution on the kitchen sink, countertops, refrigerator, and floor, use it in your bathroom and in the baby's nursery to wipe down changing tables, and wipe the telephone receiver, doorknobs, and your child's toys. Especially when someone in the family is ill, keeping your home disinfected is a good way to avoid spreading the germs to other members.

Eat plenty of fresh fruits and vegetables. Eating a well-balanced diet of fresh fruits and vegetables high in antioxidants and phytochemicals can help to maintain immune function. An antioxidant is a super nutrient that helps to repair cell damage and is vital to the body's resistance to infection. Phytochemicals are biologically active substances that give plants their color, flavor, odor, and protection against plant disease. Some phytochemicals work as potent antioxidants. Be sure to also have sufficient protein and caloric intake. (An average adult needs 45 to 55 grams of protein each day.)

Eat a varied diet. A variety of vitamins and minerals work together so you can be disease-free. For instance, vitamin E may be aggressive against viral infections and respiratory illness, while zinc fights against agents such as fungi, parasites, and viruses. Although the individual properties and functions of each nutrient are important, it is the sum of their combined effort that helps to protect and strengthen the immune system.

Stay well hydrated. Staying well hydrated with plenty of water intake throughout the day is important to detoxify the body, helping to eliminate any impurities.

A Healthy Lifestyle

Get healing sleep. Make sure you get eight hours of sleep each night. Getting enough deep sleep will allow your body tissues to rejuvenate and boost immune function. When you feel a cold coming or are feeling rundown, plan periodic rest times throughout the day to give your body a chance to regain strength.

Get plenty of exercise. During exercise, your white blood cells start to increase in number. After your workout, the number or the aggressiveness of certain immune cells such as natural killer (NK) cells increases by as much as 50 to 300 percent. When you work out consistently at a moderate pace (not high intensity), your immune system becomes a powerful weapon against viral and bacterial infections.

Chill! Avoid stressful situations, as stress wreaks havoc with hormones and may lower your immune defenses. Learn how to work periods of "time-out" or relaxation into your daily routine to ease tension and give your body time to recover.

Wash your hands frequently. While germs can be transferred through the air, ingestion, or bodily fluids, one of the biggest transportation centers for germs is your hands. However, frequent hand washing can prevent the spread of some diseases, especially if a family member has a cold or flu virus. Be sure to wash thoroughly with soap and warm water—for at least 20 seconds each time—and teach your children to do the same.

An interesting program called Operation Stop Cough was implemented at a recruit training command center in Illinois. As part of this program, recruits were instructed to wash their hands at least five times a day. After two years, the hand-washing team reported 45 percent fewer cases of respiratory ailments compared with the weekly rates of illness among recruits during the year before Operation Stop Cough started. Consider implementing a similar program in your home!

Practice prevention. You can prevent serious illnesses with regular medical checkups. Early detection and treatment work best and help you to avoid more serious health problems later on, when medication is not as effective.

People with Special Needs

Among those who should use extra caution to avoid getting sick are:
- people over age 65;

- residents of nursing homes or long-term-care facilities;
- adults and children with chronic disorders of the pulmonary or cardiovascular systems, including asthma;
- adults and children who have chronic metabolic diseases (including diabetes mellitus), renal [kidney] dysfunction, or other compromised immune function problems;
- pregnant women; and
- premature infants and newborns.

Giving Antibiotics to Food Animals Contributes to Resistance

By the Union of Concerned Scientists

According to the Union of Concerned Scientists, an advocacy group, use of antibiotics in animals raised for food is contributing to the development of antibiotic-resistant bacteria that can infect humans. They claim that the frequency of illnesses caused by bacteria acquired through food, such as campylobacter and salmonella, is increasing, and so is the frequency of antibiotic resistance among these types of bacteria. Bacteria that develop resistance to antibiotics used to treat animals, the group says, often also become resistant to chemically related antibiotics used against human infections. The Union of Concerned Scientists does not object to treating sick animals with antibiotics, but the group would like to see reduction or discontinuation of the practice of giving the drugs to healthy animals to help them use their feed more efficiently and grow more quickly. Livestock producers commonly do this to save money, but the union maintains that the goal of keeping meat prices low can be achieved just as well by making the animals' surroundings healthier, for instance by decreasing overcrowding.

If you get food poisoning, will the antibiotic prescribed by your doctor be able to fight the infection? This seems like an age of miracle drugs. Few weeks go by without a news story heralding a promising new drug or drug therapy. Ironically, concealed in the din of information about new drugs looms a health crisis growing out of the loss of old drugs.

Losing Power

Once a storehouse full of medicines such as penicillin and streptomycin could handily fight off most infections from bacteria and other microorganisms. Now, once-vulnerable bacteria have evolved resistance, and many of these drugs are losing their effectiveness. Health experts agree that there is serious danger of losing some of the most precious drugs—drugs that are most familiar as antibiotics, a subgroup of a larger group of threatened agents known as antimicrobials. Some strains of tuberculosis, for example, are now resistant to all available antimicrobial drugs. Unfortunately, tuberculosis is not the only resistant microorganism on the public health horizon.

Why are these drugs losing their power? Because they're being overused. Bacteria become resistant to antibiotics through overexposure to them. Hardy strains of the bacteria survive the exposure and pass on that resistance trait to successive generations. And they also pass the trait across to other bacteria that are unrelated, including some that cause human disease. Eventually the antibiotic wipes out all the vulnerable bacteria, and only resistant bacteria remain. Then the drug is no longer effective.

Preserving the effectiveness of antibiotics and other antimicrobials will require changes in all major areas of use: human medicine, veterinary medicine, and agriculture. But agricultural uses deserve special attention, since they provide resistant bacteria with a direct route into people's kitchens.

From Feedlot to Kitchen

Bacteria that become resistant in agricultural, particularly livestock, operations can be transferred to the general human population via food. According to a 1998 National Research Council study, *The Use of Drugs in Food Animals: Benefits and Risks*, the reported incidence of bacteria-related food-borne illness is increasing. The government is increasingly concerned about food-borne diseases caused by *Campylobacter* and *Salmonella*. As resistant strains of bacteria emerge, they have easy passage to humans—right though the grocery store.

Campylobacter, for example, is carried into kitchens on poultry and can cause illness when people eat raw or undercooked poultry meat. While this does not always cause severe illness, the Centers for Disease Control and Prevention (CDC) estimate that there are two to four million *Campylobacter* infections per year, resulting in as many as 250 deaths each year in the United States. Furthermore, about one in a thousand *Campylobacter* infections leads to Guillain-Barre syndrome, a disease that can cause paralysis. Thus, the emergence of drug-resistant *Campylobacter* would be a serious public health concern.

In fact, *Campylobacter* is becoming resistant to the fluoroquinolones, a precious class of antibiotics, as a result of agricultural use. Only recently were fluoroquinolones approved for use in poultry in the United States. Before this use, no fluoroquinolone resistance was reported in people unless they had previously taken the drugs for illness or traveled to a country that permitted their use in agriculture. But now, resistant strains are emerging in samples taken from both humans and poultry. The correlation of the emergence of resistance with the use in animal systems is important evidence that agricultural use is the culprit.

Antimicrobial use in agriculture can also compromise human therapies when bacteria develop cross-resistance—when their resistance to one drug also makes them resistant to other, related drugs. This has happened in Europe with vancomycin, one of the drugs of last resort for treating certain life-threatening infections. Data suggest that rising levels of vancomycin-resistant bacteria in hospitals may have resulted from use in agriculture of avoparcin, a drug chemically related to vancomycin. Because avoparcin and vancomycin are similar in structure, bacteria resistant to avoparcin are resistant to vancomycin as well.

Similar phenomena are apparently occurring as a result of the use of antimicrobial drugs in the United States. The effectiveness of synercid, a drug of last resort for the treatment of vancomycin-resistant infections, is threatened because of the use of virginiamycin as a growth promoter in chickens and pigs in the United States. Virginiamycin is chemically related to synercid, so that bacteria resistant to the one drug also appear to be resistant to the other.

While the links between animal agriculture and human disease are complicated and in need of additional study, evidence is strong enough for scientists and public health organizations to call for reduced use of antimicrobial growth promoters in agriculture. The

CDC has concluded that, in the United States, antimicrobial use in food animals is the *dominant* source of antibiotic resistance among food-borne pathogens.

Beefing Up Food

What can be done so that these drugs remain useful? Aren't antibiotics necessary to preserve the health of the livestock? While some uses of antibiotics in livestock operations are a matter of animal health, other uses have an economic motive. Especially troubling is their use not to cure sick animals but to promote "feed efficiency," that is, to increase the animal's weight gain per unit of feed. This so-called subtherapeutic use translates into relatively cheap meat prices at the grocery store.

But is this economic motive an essential use of these drugs? First, the economic advantage appears to be minimal. The National Research Council study estimated that a ban on such subtherapeutic use in livestock would increase per capita costs between $5 and $10 per year. That is a price most people would willingly pay to preserve a robust arsenal of medicines against infectious disease.

Second, using antimicrobial drugs is not the only way to lower meat costs. The same report suggests that adopting other methods of maintaining animal health, comfort, and well being could reduce drug use and cut costs. Such methods might include reducing overcrowding, controlling heat stress, providing vaccination to prevent disease, and using beneficial microbial cultures.

Reduction Problems

Although reducing or eliminating the use of antibiotics to promote growth is a straightforward solution to the problem of resistance, this will be difficult to achieve. Eliminating this use of antibiotics challenges the standard operating procedures of a large and powerful industry.

The subtherapeutic use of antibiotics is ingrained in livestock operations because it works. Chickens, cows, and pigs—particularly those that are not healthy to begin with—do gain weight faster when these drugs are added to their feed, and those gains translate into higher profits. In addition, livestock producers have bought into the myth that bacteria that cause illness in humans develop resistance only in medical settings. While no one denies that unwise use of antibiotics in human medicine is a source of serious resistance problems, this view has prevented recognition of one of the most attractive opportunities to cut back on these drugs—in subtherapeutic agricultural applications.

Agricultural use, much of it for growth promotion, accounts for 40 percent of the antibiotics sold in the United States. This enormous amount of drugs is delivered to animals under conditions congenial to the development of resistance. Large numbers of similar animals are raised in the concentrated facilities that characterize contemporary agriculture. Chicken houses, for example, can contain 20,000 birds. And the Environmental Protection Agency has identified 6,600 operations with at least 1,000 beef cattle or 700 dairy cattle or 2,500 hogs or 100,000 chickens.

In such large operations, antibiotics are often delivered to animals in food and water over extended periods. Bacteria are constantly being exposed to the drugs and eliminated from the populations. It is hard to imagine how resistance would not develop under these circumstances. Indeed, industrial livestock systems are hog heaven for resistant bacteria.

What's Next

The battle against emergence of antimicrobial resistance will take place on many fronts: in hospitals, in doctors' and veterinarians' offices, and on farms. The most sensible approach is to identify and reduce nonessential uses of antibiotics and reserve as many of these drugs as possible for wise use in human and veterinary medicine. Obvious nonessential uses, such as their subtherapeutic use in livestock operations, should be the first target in the effort to save antibiotics. Indeed, the CDC and the World Health Organization have called for an end to the use for growth promotion in animals of those drugs that are used to treat human disease or that are related to such medicines The Union of Concerned Scientists is taking a careful look at the health risks of industrial agriculture and will be working to reduce the subtherapeutic use of antibiotics in livestock.

Giving Antibiotics to Food Animals Does Not Contribute to Resistance

By the Animal Health Institute

The Animal Health Institute is a trade association of manufacturers of health care products given to animals, including drugs and feed additives. In the fact sheet reprinted here, the institute explains that antibiotics are used in food animals to treat, control, and prevent disease and maintain a safe food supply. It claims that all these uses of antibiotics benefit the animals, people, and the environment. Overuse and misuse of antibiotics in treating human infections is the chief cause of bacterial resistance to the drugs, it says. It maintains that agricultural producers use antibiotics judiciously, in ways that do not encourage resistance, and that antibiotic resistance among food-borne bacteria is not increasing.

Because farm animals produce a vital part of our food supply, farmers use different tools to protect and maintain the health of animals. Healthy animals are an essential first step to ensuring safe food. Some of the most important of these tools are antibiotics.

What are antibiotics?

Antibiotics are compounds produced by various living organisms, such as yeast or fungi. They inhibit the growth of or destroy certain organisms, such as bacteria. They are used to prevent and treat diseases in both animals and humans.

Why are antibiotics used in food animals?

Antibiotics are used to treat, control and prevent diseases, as well as to maintain the health of animals. They help farmers protect the whole herd or flock to ensure food safety.

Because farm animals are raised in groups, one sick animal exposes the others to illness. Antibiotics are used to treat the sick animals and also to prevent and control the spread of disease within the herd or flock. Lower amounts of antibiotics are needed to prevent and control disease than for treatment.

They also help ensure safe meat, milk and eggs. Good farm management programs that include using antibiotics reduce the amount of disease-causing bacteria that could get into the food supply.

How are antibiotics used in food animals?

Antibiotics are used for disease treatment, prevention, and control, as well as to maintain the health of animals.

Treatment: To cure animals of illnesses such as pneumonia, diarrhea and other bacterial infections and reduce the level of bacteria present. For example, when an intestinal tract disease breaks out in a swine herd, antibiotics are added to feed for up to two weeks to treat the outbreak. Similarly, farmers add antibiotics to water when chickens develop respiratory tract infections.

Prevention: To reduce the amount of potentially harmful bacteria, which can result in infections and sickness in food animals. When animals are stressed, such as when they are moved to a new environment, they become more susceptible to disease. Outbreaks can be prevented by adding an antibiotic to the feed.

Control: To stop the spread of illness to the entire herd or flock when one animal becomes sick. For example, chicks are vulnerable to a disease called colibacillosis and fatal intestinal infections, which can be controlled by adding small amounts of antibiotics to their food or water.

Health maintenance: To maintain the health of animals for better productivity. For this purpose, low doses of antibiotics, typically four to 25 grams per ton, are added to feed. This controls excess bacteria in the digestive tract of an animal, which is a normal response to a grain-based diet. Animals grow more quickly and efficiently and have better overall well-being because health maintenance antibiotics also suppress disease.

Benefits of Using Antibiotics in Food Animals

How do antibiotics protect food safety?

Consumers are protected from exposure to disease-causing bacteria through multiple layers of protection. First, antibiotics keep food safe by reducing the amount of bacteria animals carry. Then at harvest, meat processors follow strict government guidelines aimed at removing additional bacteria from the carcasses. Finally, consumers play a role because any remaining bacteria are entirely killed by proper cooking at sufficient temperatures.

Antibiotics are used to treat disease in farm animals and reduce the incidence of bacteria, which benefits all of us through healthier and safer foods Recent data show that the U.S. food supply is becoming safer than ever before.

Who benefits from using antibiotics in farm animals?

Animals, people and the environment all benefit from proper antibiotic use.

Antibiotics help ensure an animal's well-being by lowering the incidence of sickness and death within a herd or flock. They are used to treat sick animals while also managing disease in a herd or flock before it becomes widespread. When used for health maintenance, antibiotics help animals grow more efficiently by controlling overgrowth of bacteria in their intestines, which is a normal response to their grain-based diet. Health maintenance, also called growth promotion, provides an added benefit of disease suppression.

People benefit from antibiotics because healthy animals help reduce food borne illness. They also ensure that as the world population grows, there will be enough protein to feed everyone because antibiotics promote health and productivity. Meat, milk and eggs are sources of high-quality protein in a balanced diet.

The environment wins, too. Antibiotics allow farmers to use less land and water to achieve current production levels of meat and poultry, thus protecting precious resources. In addition, antibiotics allow farmers to produce animals with less manure to dispose of, as well as less feed, cropland, and water needed.

What does resistance mean?

Resistance is a natural biological defense bacteria use to survive. This can be either *acquired* through genetic changes after bacteria have been exposed to an antibiotic, or *intrinsic*, meaning that some bacteria are naturally resistant to certain antibiotics. For example, penicillin has never been effective in treating *Salmonella.*

Every time a human or animal patient takes an antibiotic for a bacterial infection, the drug may kill most of the bacteria. But a few tenacious germs may survive by mutating or acquiring resistance genes from other bacteria. These surviving genes can multiply quickly, creating drug-resistant strains. The presence of these strains may mean that the patient's next infection will not respond to the first-choice antibiotic therapy. Also, the resistant bacteria may be transmitted to others in the patient's community.

What causes resistance?

Many factors lead to antibiotic resistance:

- Bacteria can develop resistance because they contain genetic material that allow them to grow and reproduce more resistant bacteria.
- Some bacteria are naturally resistant to certain antibiotics.
- Resistance can be transferred from one type of bacteria to another.
- Bacteria can develop resistance over time by random changes in their genetic makeup, or mutation.

Many scientists believe dependence on and misuse of antibiotics in human medicine is the primary cause of resistance. One example of this is when antibiotics are prescribed for viral infection, despite the fact that antibiotics do not work on viruses. Or, people sometimes fail to finish an antibiotic prescription when they start feeling better, which can allow stubborn bacteria to survive, grow stronger and develop resistance. Some patients also take leftover antibiotics for an illness it was not prescribed for. These antibiotic misuses can all increase the probability of developing resistance.

Using Antibiotics in Food Animals Is Safe

Does using antibiotics in animals pose a public health issue?

The potential exists for resistant bacteria in animals to transfer to humans. However, largely due to management measures put in place to prevent such a transfer, there is no evidence that this potential transfer is actually taking place. The animal health industry and health and government organizations have developed judicious antibiotic use guidelines and quality assurance programs for food animals to prevent resistance transfer from harming public health.

In addition, surveillance of resistant bacteria helps us monitor public health and identify problems in both human and veterinary medicine. The Food and Drug Administration (FDA), Centers for Disease Control and Prevention (CDC), and the U.S. Department of Agriculture (USDA) work together to monitor levels of resistant food borne pathogens in both humans and animals. This surveillance program, the National Antimicrobial Resistance Monitoring System (NARMS), has data that show resistance among animal pathogens is relatively stable. In humans, recent data show that the incidence of resistant food borne pathogens is declining.

What is the process to ensure our food is safe?

The U.S. has one of the world's safest food supplies, and antibiotics are one of many important tools farmers use to produce high quality and safe food products. Animal antibiotics undergo a rigorous approval process before reaching farmers. They only enter the marketplace after extensive data has been presented to the FDA Center for Veterinary Medicine (CVM) to demonstrate their safety. After approval of the antibiotic, monitoring and surveillance continues to ensure the drug's effectiveness.

Drug manufacturers, with FDA oversight, establish withdrawal times so that animals are not harvested before antibiotics are metabolized. They also label products with dosage requirements so that animals receive the appropriate amount of antibiotic, thus discouraging the development of resistant bacteria.

Finally, judicious use guidelines and education programs, similar to successful programs initiated in human medicine, help the agriculture industry safely and responsibly use antibiotics.

How much are antibiotics used in food animals?

Antibiotics are used in minute doses in farm animals' water or feed to protect them from disease or illness. The average amount in medicated feed is four to 25 grams per ton of feed. In addition, the majority of antibiotics used in the United States are for preventing and curing illness, with only 13% for health maintenance, also called growth promotion.

To keep the amount of antibiotic use in perspective, we must consider that there are many more food-producing animals than humans. In fact, there are approximately 282 million people versus:
- 7.5 billion chickens
- 292 million turkeys
- 109 million cattle
- 92 million pigs
- 7 million sheep

History of Use and Research

Since 1951 when the FDA first approved antibiotics as feed additives for farm animals, antibiotics have helped keep our nation's farm animals in good health. Animal antibiotics are given a stringent, science-based regulatory review by the FDA before they are approved. The USDA's Food Safety and Inspection Service (FSIS) both continually monitor antibiotic use in food animals. Food animal producers and veterinarians rely on these agencies to ensure safety, and abide by their rules.

For more than 40 years, scientists have meticulously studied the issue of antibiotics to ensure that they do not threaten human health.

Antibiotics Will Soon Be Useless

By Carlos F. Amabile-Cuevas

Bacteria's development of resistance to antibiotics is so inevitable, Carlos F. Amabile-Cuevas believes, that the drugs—and the whole concept of treating infectious disease on which they are based—are bound to become useless. Amabile-Cuevas founded and heads Fundacion Lusara in Mexico City, a research institute that studies antibiotic resistance and related problems in molecular biology. In this selection, Amabile-Cuevas describes several mechanisms by which resistance can develop and discusses the complex evolution of resistance. He points out that new forms of resistance and resistance to new groups of drugs have developed in the last fifteen years, sometimes side by side with increased virulence (ability to cause disease). He says that developing new types of antibiotics and teaching physicians and consumers to use the drugs carefully are both necessary to slow the further development of resistance, but he doubts that these efforts can completely solve the problem. Instead, he believes, medicine will enter a "post-antibiotic era" and will have to find new ways to minimize infectious disease. According to Amabile-Cuevas, these may include reducing bacterial virulence, boosting the immune system with vaccines, and creating drugs that attack genetic elements that transfer resistance.

B acterial infections have been a scourge on humankind for millennia. Plague, tuberculosis, wound infections and typhoid fever have caused historical as well as personal tragedies. No wonder, then, that antibiotics were greeted as miracle drugs. For a few decades the success of antibiotic therapies was remarkable, but enthusiasm for them led to abuses. Observers disregarded the early emergence of resistant bacteria; a number of new antibiotics were still being discovered, suggesting that effective drugs would always be available. With infections deemed under control, pharmaceutical companies lost interest in developing new antibiotics.

After decades of complacency and just 50 years after the first clinical use of an antibiotic, penicillin, the public health threat posed by antibiotic resistance finally gained widespread attention. Resistance made the cover of *Time* and *Newsweek* in the early 1990s; [in 2003] most people know that antibiotics can fail. Over nearly 20 years, from the early 1980s to the late 1990s, not a single truly new antibiotic was introduced into clinical use. Barely a trickle reached the market [between 1999 and 2003]. Meanwhile, resistance keeps evolving, and drugs are rapidly losing their efficacy, resulting in increased treatment costs, loss of labor time and, of course worst of all, lost lives. My colleagues and I reviewed how bacteria evolve so quickly towards resistance [in 1995.] Here I will discuss new discoveries on the biology of resistance, as well as efforts to either restrain or circumvent resistant organisms. In the struggle against antibiotic resistance, science is providing useful tools, and physicians are slowly realizing that antibiotics are simultaneously powerful and dangerous drugs. Ultimately, though, we will all need to change the way we deal with bacteria in the coming "post-antibiotic era."

Ways Bacteria Resist Antibiotics

Antibiotics are compounds that kill or at least inhibit the growth of bacterial cells, without harming the patient. No single antibiotic can kill or inhibit all bacteria. Natural penicillin and macrolides, such as erythromycin, for instance, cannot penetrate into the gut bacterium *Escherichia coli* and its relatives; only a handful of drugs work against the almost impermeable *Mycobacterium tuberculosis*, which causes tuberculosis. The intrinsic resistance of bacteria defines the spectrum of each antibiotic; wide-spectrum antibiotics are effective against a variety of germs, whereas narrow-spectrum antibiotics only control a few species. But the antibiotic resistance we normally speak about refers to cases in which organisms that were originally killed by a certain drug suddenly keep growing in its presence. When a concentration of antibiotic safely attainable in the blood and tissues of a patient no longer affects an organism, we say the strain has become resistant.

The first explanation for resistance was that mutations, small changes in the genetic information, of a bacterial cell, somehow prevented an antibiotic from acting on it. Certainly, many resistant organisms arose through the acquisition of spontaneous mutations; this is particularly true for germs causing tuberculosis. But, unexpectedly, genes conferring resistance rapidly emerged and accumulated, quickly yielding multi-resistant bacteria—that is, strains resistant to three or more antibiotics. Also, some bacteria were found to have the same resistance genes as those found in species that naturally produce antibiotics. (Most antibiotics are obtained from various species of soil bacteria, which have been producing these compounds for millions of years.)

It became clear [around 1993] that bacteria can exchange genes, a process known as horizontal gene transfer. In this way, a mutation conferring antibiotic resistance can be acquired by neighboring bacteria, even if they are very distantly related species. The resistance genes can spread from mutants or even directly from antibiotic-producing species. Furthermore, such genes can accumulate in a single cell, resulting in multi-resistant germs.

Bacteria often carry the resistance genes in small DNA molecules called plasmids, which act as genetic "supplements" to the core genome. Exchanging these supplements is easier than mobilizing genes in the genome, just as it would be easier to borrow a magazine rather than a large, expensive book from a friend. Genes conferring other dangerous traits, such as virulence, are also often found in plasmids.

In addition to specific antibiotic-resistance genes, bacteria have defense mechanisms that prevent the entrance of noxious compounds or that pump them out of the cell. These mechanisms are activated in response to particular chemical signals and can make a population of germs transiently resistant to multiple drugs. In *E. coli* at least two of these mechanisms are known. The mar regulon, discovered by Stuart Levy's group at Tufts University, is a set of genes that is activated by a single regulatory protein that leads to multiple antibiotic resistance. The sox regulon, described by Bruce Demple's team at Harvard, is a somewhat overlapping set of genes that is activated by superoxide radicals. The activating signals for such regulons are very diverse—ranging from salicylate, the active compound of aspirin, to superoxide radicals, released by white blood cells to kill invading bacteria. Ana Fuentes in my lab discovered that even mercury, at concentrations similar to those released from "silver" dental fillings while chewing, can activate the sox system. Once activated, these systems protect bacteria from a number of antibiotics; mutations that keep any of these systems permanently activated result in permanent multi-resistance.

Yet another strategy allows bacteria to survive antibiotics. The cells often grow in complex, multi-layered, multi-species consortia—what one might call "cities of microbes." These aggregations are called biofilms, a term coined by William Costerton of Montana State University. Small subpopulations within these consortia are able to withstand the presence of antimicrobial agents and can resume growing once the agent is gone. This persistence, rather than actual resistance, is responsible for antibiotic treatment failures, especially when the biofilm is attached to foreign bodies, such as prostheses or catheters. The precise mechanism of this persistence is not well known, but slow diffusion of an antibiotic across the biofilm may give some cells enough time to activate environmental stress responses, such as the mar or sox mechanisms. Also, biofilms might be ideal places for horizontal gene mobilization, allowing resistance genes to be transferred and expressed rapidly. [In 2002], Eliana Drenkard and Frederick M. Ausubel at Harvard Medical School identified a protein of *Pseudomonas aeruginosa* that regulates both biofilm formation and a switch between antibiotic resistance and susceptibility. Fabrizio Delissalde in my lab discovered [in 2000] that among strains of *P. aeruginosa* causing infections in hospitalized patients, the greater the ability to produce biofilm, the fewer the drug-specific resistance genes in the strain. We suppose that the protection from forming biofilms is enough for these bacteria to survive in hospitals, where antibiotics are ubiquitous.

In addition, we were surprised to find that biofilm-forming strains are no more likely to carry plasmids than strains that don't form biofilms, even though gene mobilization has been proven to occur within biofilms and, indeed, conjugation, a powerful gene-mobilizing mechanism, enables the formation of biofilms in *E. coli*.

New Examples of Resistance

One of the most disturbing new cases of resistance was the recent isolation of a strain of *Staphylococcus aureus*, also known as "golden staph" for the color of its colonies, that is resistant to vancomycin. This drug is regarded as the final weapon against infections caused by enterococci and staphylococci, two groups of organisms that often cause infections in hospitalized patients, Vancomycin-resistant enterococci are already a public health problem, but until [the early 2000s] the drug was always effective against the golden staph. Then in July 2002, the Centers for Disease Control and Prevention confirmed the isolation of the first vancomycin-resistant strain of this dangerous germ from a Michigan man undergoing chronic renal dialysis [artificial blood filtration given to people whose kidneys have failed]. Some staph strains were already known to have reduced susceptibility to vancomycin, but, reassuringly, experimental attempts to introduce vancomycin-resistance genes into *Staphylococcus aureus* had failed because the genes became unstable and were quickly lost. However, it seems that after continuous exposure some germs can keep such genes. It is likely that under the enormous pressure applied by the reckless use of antibiotics, the dangerous new strain gained not only the resistance trait but also the capability to somehow retain it.

An interesting sidelight to this dire situation is how vancomycin-resistance genes evolve. A bacterium needs several genes to circumvent the effect of vancomycin; the genes are all arranged together and are activated simultaneously, in what is known as an operon. But genes in the vancomycin-resistance operon seem to come from different sources, as revealed in DNA sequence analysis by Patrice Courvalin of the Institut Pasteur. Enterococci and staphylococci seem to have a particular ability to shuffle and reassemble DNA sequences.

Other antibiotic families are also in jeopardy. Fluoroquinolones are a family of drugs that have been intensely exploited during the last 15 years. One of the first drugs in the group was . . . ciprofloxacin, somehow erroneously supposed the only drug effective against the anthrax bacterium, *Bacillus anthracis*, [which became famous] during the terrorist mailings of that germ [in late 2001]. . . . Newer generations of fluoroquinolones are now available and are being used against bacteria, such as *Streptococcus pneumoniae*, that cause respiratory infections and are increasingly resistant to penicillin and erythromycin. One interesting feature of fluoroquinolones is that resistance to them results mainly from mutations in genes encoding enzymes that the antibiotics target; these genes are difficult to transfer horizontally. But in 2002, John Tran and George Jacoby of Lahey Clinic in Burlington, Massachusetts, described the first fluoroquinolone-resistant mechanism caused by a plasmid in gram-negative bacteria such as *E. coli*. A protein encoded by the plasmid they discovered can protect the target enzyme from the action of the drugs. It is still [too] early to know how common this mechanism is among fluoroquinolone-resistant bacteria and how successful it can be; however, it seems a new path for the horizontal transmission of genes enabling bacterial survival.

Carbapenems, mainly imipenem and meropenem, are two very wide-spectrum antibiotics, used only in hospitals to treat serious infections. Until recently, these drugs were invaluable against infections caused by multi-resistant bacteria, such as opportunistic pathogens, which are often around but typically only seize the chance to cause infection when a patient has a wound, an invasive medical procedure or a weakened immune system; examples of such bacteria are *Pseudomonas aeruginosa* and *Klebsiella pneumoniae*. But now isolates of these species are becoming resistant at alarming rates.

Some strains have an old, rare enzyme capable of destroying the antibiotic molecule. An increasing number of strains have enzymes that in earlier forms inactivated other, related drugs but have evolved to quell antibiotics that are presently the last hope against some serious hospital infections.

The Evolution of Resistance

To understand the evolution of resistance, it is worth considering some conceptual proposals. Jack Heinemann of the University of Canterbury in New Zealand, an expert in horizontal gene transfer, proposes, that the evolution of resistance strongly depends on the biology of bacterial plasmids. [Around 1983] Ken Gerdes, at the Technical University of Denmark, discovered an intricate system that prevents the survival of bacterial cells that spontaneously lose their plasmids. A so-called post-segregational killing (psk) system consists of two genes in the plasmid, one encoding a toxic protein and the other an RNA that prevents the expression of that protein. While the plasmid is in the cell, both genes are transcribed, but the toxic protein is never produced. But when the plasmid is lost, the messenger RNA that encodes the toxic protein outlives the inhibitor (antisense) RNA, so the protein is produced and the cell dies. This system ensures the survival of a plasmid within its bacterial host, since any cells that lose the plasmid will quickly be culled from the population. Heinemann proposes that antibiotics act as an external toxin in an analogous system, where resistance genes provide the antidote. If the plasmid is lost, the antibiotic kills the cell; antibiotics are therefore driving the evolution and spread of plasmids.

It is important to remember that most antibiotics are in no way new to bacteria; Julian Davies at the University of British Columbia even proposes that antibiotics could be some of the oldest biomolecules. Among clinical isolates [of bacteria] stored from before the antibiotic era, almost none are resistant to antibiotics. But based on sequence analysis, Miriam Barlow and Barry G. Hall of the University of Rochester have proposed that genes for enzymes that inactivate beta-lactam antibiotics such as penicillin (which inhibit bacterial cell-wall synthesis), or at least enzymes very closely related to them, have been in plasmids for millions of years. It therefore appears likely that interactions between plasmids and antibiotics are much older than humankind itself and that the only thing we did when releasing massive amounts of antibiotics was to make such interactions a much more common phenomenon.

In the field of antibiotic resistance, one deeply disturbing issue concerns how resistance relates to the ability of bacteria to cause disease—that is, their virulence. It's frightening to think that more resistant bacteria might also be particularly virulent, but we may be creating just such germs. Plasmids containing both resistance and virulence genes have been described since the 1970s. Microbiologists are now finding virulence and resistance genes in other, smaller kinds of mobile genetic elements, such as integrons and gene cassettes, which can rearrange to create dangerous combinations. When these genes are linked, abusing antibiotics can select not only resistant bacteria but also more virulent ones.

It is also becoming apparent that virulence and resistance can often be the outcomes of the same mechanism. Pumps that expel noxious compounds from bacterial cells can detoxify the cells from bile salts, allowing them to survive in the intestinal tract as well as resist antibiotics. Mechanisms that protect bacteria from free-radical molecules generated by immune cells can also protect them from antibacterial drugs. From the epidemiological point of view, a more resistant bacterium will be a more successful invader and will have more chances to spread through contagion, since patients will remain sick for longer periods of time. In this way, resistant bacteria are not only more difficult to control, but also more harmful.

"New" and "Semi-New" Antibiotics

Pharmaceutical companies are now recovering from nearly 20 years of not looking for new antibacterial compounds. Somehow, during the 1970s and 1980s, the notion that infectious diseases were defeated even diffused into research and development teams. Also, some proposed that the more promising business for the pharmaceutical industry lay in the treatment of chronic diseases, which require continuous medication, rather than infections, which are quickly resolved. In any case, until recently, the only "new" antibiotics were slightly modified forms of old chemicals. Such tinkering gave rise to the third and fourth generations of cephalosporins, originally discovered in the 1950s; the second generation of aminoglycosides, originating from the 1940s; and newer versions of macrolides discovered 50 years ago. The last family developed in the first wave of antibiotic discovery were quinolones, originally patented in the 1960s; their improved derivatives, the fluoroquinolones, first came on the market in the early 1980s. This strategy of improving old drugs is still generating many "semi-new" antibiotics. Fortunately, some entirely new families of antibiotics are now also reaching the market.

Among the truly new drugs are oxazolidinones, such as Linezolid and everninomycins. These drugs are aimed at infections caused by gram-positive pathogens, such as pneumococci, enterococci and the golden staph and its relatives. Many of these organisms cause infections in hospitalized patients. These paradoxical sorts of diseases, which a patient acquires while being treated for another illness, can be very severe. Drugs against these life-threatening infections are certainly needed. But infections caused by gut bacteria (most of them gram-negative) are not receiving adequate attention, and resistance among this group is growing continuously.

Drugs for the treatment of tuberculosis are also certainly needed. For many years, almost no effort was made to find new anti-TB drugs for what was considered a vanishing disease, at least in developed countries. But after an outbreak in New York City in the early 1990s, where nearly 10 percent of the cases proved resistant to two or more drugs, TB regained the attention of the public and, one hopes, of pharmaceutical companies. *Mycobacterium tuberculosis* happens to be a particularly tough germ; it is covered by several layers of cell wall, including one similar to wax, which prevent many drugs from penetrating into the cell.

It is further protected from many antibiotics because it grows within immune system cells, and it grows slowly, so treatments need to be maintained for long periods—up to six months on average. Also, it has marketing disadvantages; although TB kills 2 million people a year worldwide, it is mainly a disease of the poor. Until [the 1990s] however, the four or five anti-TB agents were still useful, especially when used in combinations of two or three. But as multi-resistance rises, we are running out of options. Although a $25 million donation [made by] the Bill and Melinda Gates Foundation [in 1999] and other funds are becoming available for tuberculosis research, the money available pales in comparison to the $350 million typically expended by pharmaceutical companies to develop each new antibiotic.

Promoting Rational Use of Antibiotics

Since antibiotic abuse has caused rising antibiotic resistance, the prudent use of antibiotics as an antidote to this trend has been gaining more and more attention. An estimated 90 to 180 million kilograms of antibiotics are used yearly, according to Richard Wise of the City Hospital NHS [National Health Service] Trust at Birmingham, U.K. Considering that such an amount would provide roughly 25 billion full treatment courses—four per year for every human being—it seems necessary to cut this number. Some important battles have been won in the fight for rational use. Antibiotic sales are diminishing worldwide, although the sale of all other kinds of drugs is increasing. The efforts of the Alliance for the Prudent Use of Antibiotics (APUA), headed by Stuart Levy of Tufts University, have won the attention of U.S. lawmakers, and the agricultural use of antibiotics is now facing more obstacles.

Antibiotics have been added to the food of farm animals for decades as "growth promoters." Some actual growth promotion along with reduced frequencies of infections among animals yield a small profit for farmers, and huge ones for pharmaceutical companies. (About 10 times more antibiotics are used in the United States for agriculture than to treat human infections, according to the Food and Drug Administration [FDA]). But it has been well documented that the use of antibiotics leads to resistance among bacteria in animals, and these resistant germs can be transmitted to humans through foodstuff. Therefore, it would be a significant victory to have antibiotics removed from animals' food. The

Preservation of Antibiotics for Human Treatment Act of 2002 was introduced to Congress, and the FDA issued a resolution aiming to limit the use of antibiotics as routine additives to animal feed and water. Also, major chicken producers are significantly reducing the use of antibiotics in healthy animals, as large fast-food companies said [in early 2002] they will not buy chickens fed medically important antibiotics. In this regard, the United States is behind Europe; [in 2002] the European Court of First Instance upheld a 1998 decision by the EU [European Union] Council of Ministers to ban the use of several antibiotics in animal feed.

These encouraging advances have been made despite the gigantic disproportion between the few funds and people devoted to the rational use of antibiotics versus the resources of pharmaceutical companies dedicated to selling more drugs. This is not meant to attack the pharmaceutical industry: They develop new antibiotics at great cost and must sell those antibiotics as much as possible to profit from them. They also face a deadline—the lifespan of patent coverage before others can manufacture and sell the compound without investing in research. Hence, multi-million dollar efforts are conducted to push for clinical and non-clinical use of antibiotics, often resulting in abuse.

Efforts aimed at promoting the rational use of antibiotics rely mostly on academic activities, such as conferences and publications; these have to compete with expensive advertising and other aggressive strategies used to push physicians into prescribing all sort of antibiotics. For a global usage-reduction strategy to work, it is vital that pharmaceutical companies get involved. Researchers must provide evidence that the fast emergence of resistance is not good for business. Some have suggested that extending the lifespan of antibiotic patents will allow pharmaceutical companies more time to sell their products, diminishing the pressure to promote prescriptions. In any case, if rational-use advocates fail to consider the interest of the pharmaceutical industry they will always have to fight uphill.

In many developing countries there is no need for a physician's prescription to buy antibiotics. In Mexico City, for instance, around 30 percent of all antibiotics sold at drugstores are sold without a prescription. But banning such sales is not an uncomplicated good; a significant fraction of the population lacks medical services, and self-prescription may be the only way these people can have access to drugs. It is difficult to assess how large the impact of this self-prescription is on increased antibiotic resistance and to weigh that risk against the risk from limiting access to antibiotics among people who lack formal medical care. Also, self-prescription is practiced in developed countries; a [July 2002] report from Brandon Goff and coworkers at the Pentagon Clinic found that soldiers often buy and use antibiotics from the fish medication aisle of pet stores, which freely sell many antibiotics, such as erythromycin, kanamycin, penicillin, ampicillin, tetracycline, a variety of sulfonamides, nitrofurazone and metronidazole.

Is Rational Use the Solution?

An enormous amount of evidence shows that the human use of antibiotics created the selective pressure that led to the emergence and early spread of resistance among bacteria. However, it is also clear that once resistance is established in a bacterial population, it won't disappear easily. This came as a surprise to many researchers, because they believed resistance genes always represent a cost to those bacteria bearing them, one that is too high when antibiotics are not present. However, either the burden of carrying resistance traits is not that high or resistance genes are being maintained through other, essentially unknown mechanisms. In now-classic experiments, Judith E. Bouma and Richard E. Lenski at the University of California, Irvine showed that, in the absence of antibiotics, resistance plasmids and their bacterial hosts co-evolve in such a way that, after several generations, they grow better than a strain that lacks the plasmid or a strain with a new association between plasmid and host. Dan Andersson and his team at the Swedish Institute for Infectious Disease Control and Uppsala University recently showed that additional mutations can compensate for any cost on bacterial fitness imposed by the mutations conferring resistance, without compromising the resistance.

In addition, antibiotic resistance genes are often physically linked to genes encoding other useful traits, as when several different genes are carried on the same plasmid; the selective pressure that favors one of the traits cross-selects for others close to it. Resistance to disinfectants and other toxic compounds is often linked to antibiotic-resistance genes; therefore, such compounds can cross-select for antibiotic-resistant bacteria. Also, some genes provide protection not only from antibiotics but also from other kinds of environmental stress. For example, even an air pollutant like ozone might select for antibiotic-resistant bacteria, as Gabriela Jimenez-Arribas and Veronica Leautaud showed in our lab in collaborative work with Bruce Demple of Harvard.

Appreciating how hard it is to lose resistance is an important part of realizing the real reach of programs that encourage the rational use of antibiotics. Of course, we must move towards rational antibiotic use to prevent the emergence of more resistance genes and more resistant organisms. But rational use will not do away with resistant strains. My lab explored an interesting example of this paradox. The commercial blockade on Cuba, along with the fall of socialism in Eastern Europe, has made antibiotics, particularly newer ones, a very scarce commodity on the island. The use of the drugs has been strictly controlled since 1990. Cuban scientists report that antibiotic resistance among disease-causing bacteria is receding. But my colleagues Javier Diaz-Mejia and Alejandro Carbajal-Saucedo found that the degree of resistance among the harmless bacteria in the mouths of Cubans is about equal to that found in the mouths of Mexicans, even though antibiotics are sold without prescription in Mexico and are also used in agriculture. Since benign bacteria often act as reservoirs of resistance genes that can be transferred to virulent bacteria, it was surprising to find such high frequencies of resistance after 10 years of severe usage reduction in Cuba. This, along with a wealth of other reports, indicates that resistance seldom disappears and that what we can expect from rational-use policies will be the slower emergence of new resistance mechanisms, but not a reversal of the trend nor a solution to the resistance problem. Of course, rational use of old and new drugs is vital, but it must be regarded as just one part of a larger strategy.

The Search for New Drugs

Until recently, the search for new antibiotics was performed using 40-year-old strategies: Compounds from several sources—from crude extracts of plants, animals and bacteria to synthetic molecules—were tested for the ability to inhibit the growth of selected microorganisms. Those compounds that showed some potential were further analyzed to isolate the active component and to look into its stability and toxicity. The few promising molecules or their slightly modified forms were then brought into pre-clinical and then clinical trials. The mechanism of action and other important details of their interactions with bacteria and humans have often been discovered only after the drugs come into use. This strategy, undoubtedly successful in many ways, missed important candidates that were unstable or toxic, or just did not penetrate to their targets in bacterial cells. Such problems could have been fixed with chemical manipulations. Also, only compounds that killed or completely inhibited bacteria growth were detected; this screening would miss those compounds able to limit the ability of virulent bacteria to harm us without damaging the bacteria.

During the late 1980s and early 1990s, a new approach to drug discovery became available—chemical design. Databases filled with the chemical structure of known drugs and their biological activities could be used to design new candidates. Such designs were synthesized in chemical labs and then tested for the expected biological activity. Although this would seem a more directed search, trying to incorporate additional data, such as the pharmacological behavior and toxicity of known compounds, made this a formidable task.

[In the 2000s], the full genome sequences of a growing number of pathogenic bacteria are becoming available, another process is starting to become possible. DNA and protein sequences can reveal potential drug targets in virulent bacteria. These targets need to be essential for bacterial survival or virulence and, simultaneously, absent in the genomes of humans and other mammals. New computational methods are also helping to infer the function of proteins solely from the genome sequence that codes for them. Selected targets need to be validated in the lab, and then an easy controlled assay must be developed to screen for compounds that inhibit the protein's specific activity. Candidate compounds can be modified to improve their penetration and stability, or to diminish their toxicity, if any. The search can be directed toward widespectrum agents by finding targets shared by a large number of bacterial species or toward narrow-spectrum ones by looking into targets found only in a few organisms. Advances in miniaturization and robotics allow thousands of compounds to be screened in a few days or hours using minute quantities of experimental compounds. Meanwhile, combinatorial chemistry can provide a larger number of candidate drugs much faster. New antibacterial agents that arose partially from these strategies are on their way to clinical trials; inhibitors of peptide deformylase enzymes, essential to life for most bacteria but absent or not vital to humans, are being studied by Versicolor and British Biotech; and ACP-reductase, involved in the synthesis of bacterial fatty acids, is an attractive target to Glaxo-SmithKline.

Different Ways to Fight Infection

But perhaps the very way we fight infection should be reconsidered. As in other aspects of our social behavior, we identify sometimes-annoying creatures as mortal enemies and are determined to annihilate them. Even when these efforts prove futile, we insist on the approach, as in the fad of including disinfectants in numerous household products. The abuse of antibiotics is another instance of this ill-conceived strategy. A more promising avenue may be the idea of inhibiting virulence instead of killing germs outright. This is an old idea, but new technologies such as microarray profiling are making this a more feasible goal. Back in the 1970s, compounds that could inhibit the adhesion of virulent bacteria to a tissue, believed to be the first step in infection, yielded inconsistent results. Now, new technologies can detect specific genes that are switched on during infection and which are essential for a successful infection. The products of these genes are ideal targets for new anti-infection drugs. These drugs might have important advantages compared to current antibiotics. Since they do not kill bacteria, selection of resistant strains could be much slower. Also, they will only affect virulent bacteria, diminishing the risk of selecting resistance among normal flora, which, in turn, can transfer those genes to pathogenic germs later.

Despite the promise of this approach, assessing which genes are suitable targets and even designing the clinical tests for their efficacy are proving to be enormous challenges. Virulence genes are often switched off in ordinary laboratory conditions. Furthermore, inhibiting virulence might be a powerful way to prevent an infection, but not to get rid of an already established pathogen. For these strategies to work, a number of problems must be solved. Testing of the efficacy of such non-lethal drugs will require entirely new techniques, since it won't be possible to simply see if bacteria grow or not. Drugs that inhibit only the virulence trait will require specific tests that are more difficult to set up and more expensive. Also, since virulence inhibitors are likely to have a narrow spectrum, affecting only a few related organisms, it would be necessary to improve methods of ascertaining the types of infection in a patient, a task that now often takes a couple of days.

Genome sequencing efforts can also fuel the search for vaccines. Preventing infectious disease is often much better than trying to fight an established illness. The sequencing of the immense genome of *Neisseria meningitidis*, which causes meningitis, in 2000 allowed the identification of candidates for a vaccine against this organism. Although a vaccine has yet to be developed from such efforts, the approach seems very promising where others have failed.

My colleagues and I have taken another approach—searching for compounds that circumvent resistance. This is hardly a new approach; the compounds clavulanic acid and sulbactam have been successfully used for some years to inhibit the enzymes that resistant bacteria use to destroy some antibiotics. One idea for fighting antibiotic resistance has been to target the plasmids that contain the resistance genes. Based on old reports that ascorbic acid (vitamin C) can suppress the replication of the bacterial viruses known as bacteriophages and knowing that the DNA in bacteriophages is similar to plasmid DNA, we tested the anti-plasmid activity of ascorbic acid—with good results. Looking into compounds that have similar activities, we have found a handful of interesting drug candidates. This approach may only be useful for a few plasmid-bacteria combinations, but even a narrow-spectrum drug could prove valuable when treating critically ill patients. Also, as some virulence determinants exclusively reside on plasmids, affecting their expression or stability could be beneficial. For instance, the main difference between dangerous *Bacillus anthracis*, the causative agent of anthrax, and the almost-innocuous *Bacillus cereus*, a soil bacterium, is a virulence plasmid. This plasmid could make an extraordinary target for research.

Lessons from a Lost Battle

Along with regulating antibiotic use and searching for new drugs and even new strategies to fight infections, it is necessary to improve the education of health-care personnel. As much as half of medically prescribed antibiotics are unnecessary, a remnant of the deeply wrong notion that antibiotics are drugs that, if not always beneficial, are at least not harmful. Perhaps on the level of a single patient, this view can still hold, since most antibiotics have few side effects, but from the public health perspective antibiotic abuse is extremely dangerous and also expensive, since the consequences of antibiotic resistance are estimated to cost $4 billion to $5 billion annually in the United States, according to the FDA. Many physicians prescribe antibiotics with a just-in-case philosophy, for example doling out "preventive" antibiotics for travelers' diarrhea. In many hospitals, third-generation cephalosporins are predominantly used in emergency rooms when the existence of infections has not even been established. Many such interventions are of dubious efficacy and certainly pose an additional pressure favoring resistant bacteria.

Physicians and medical students do not often fully realize the intricacies of evolution and natural selection, let alone the powerful mechanisms that bacteria have to face aggression and stress. This is completely understandable, since doctors already have to deal with hundreds of organs, diseases, drugs and procedures. But in order to sway medical personnel toward the rational use of antibiotics, it is imperative to teach them the basics of resistance from an evolutionary point of view. Ideally, such education should be as appealing as the pharmaceutical ads used to push doctors towards antibiotic prescription. My colleague Isabel Nivon-Bolan designed a card game that explains dynamically how resistance genes are acquired or activated and how antibiotics and other agents can favor resistant organisms. This game does not require previous knowledge of bacteria, infections or antibiotics and is actually fun as well as illuminating, as we've heard from medical and biology students. Approaches like this can transform the attitude of both lay people and physicians toward antibiotics.

We must assume that the war against bacteria, as it was conceived during the antibiotic era, is already lost. We must necessarily move into a post-antibiotic era. As we do so, we should adjust our attitude against these much older and much more abundant organisms that share the planet with us. We know now how tough bacteria are as enemies, but we have new data on the molecular mechanisms we can use to tame them. Let's hope we all—patients, physicians, researchers and pharmaceutical companies—quickly learn the lessons of the lost battle.

An Alternative to Antibiotics

By Angela Pirisi

One possible alternative to antibiotics for controlling infectious disease, says Angela Pirisi, a Toronto (Canada) freelance writer who specializes in medicine and health subjects, is bacteriophages ("phages" for short)—viruses that infect only bacteria. Unlike antibiotics, she writes, phages target only particular types of bacteria, so helpful bacteria in, say, the digestive system will not be killed along with harmful ones. Furthermore, phages can multiply and evolve just as fast as bacteria can, so resistance to them can be minimized, she points out. Pirisi notes that poorly carried out experiments early in the twentieth century gave bacteriophage therapy a bad reputation in Western medicine, but she claims that it has been widely accepted in eastern Europe for decades. Several problems remain to be solved, she admits, including the need for precise identification of the bacteria causing a disease and the fact that the body tends to destroy phages before they can do their work. Pirisi maintains, however, that new research seems likely to overcome these obstacles. Phages probably will not completely replace antibiotics, according to the sources Pirisi quotes, but they could be a valuable supplement to the drugs.

As antibiotic-resistant bacteria continue to threaten standard therapies against bacterial infections, a new breed of antimicrobials may be on the horizon. Many researchers believe that bacteriophages—viruses that only infect bacteria—are a promising potential therapy for bacterial disease treatment.

Phage therapy boasts several advantages over traditional antibiotics. "Yeast infection and diarrhoea are frequent side effects of antibacterial therapy because the beneficial bacteria of the genital tract and intestines are also killed, disrupting the ecology and enabling other pathogens to grow out and cause disease," explains Paul Gulig (University of Florida, Gainesville, FL, USA). However, bacteriophages target specific bacterial strains, thus sparing patients from the side effects caused by destroying natural flora.

Another positive aspect of phages is their capacity for exponential growth. Essentially, phages closely follow the course of bacterial growth and presence, multiplying alongside bacteria, and disappearing once the bacteria have gone. Even though bacterial resistance is a concern, unlike antibiotics, phages can mutate in step with evolving bacteria. Also if bacteria become resistant to one phage, there is a natural abundance of phage species, which could attack even new resistant strains.

Richard Carlton, president of Exponential Biotherapies (Port Washington, NY, USA), explains, "one great thing about phages is that mutations that enable bacteria to resist antibiotics do not enable the bacteria to resist the phage, and vice versa." That's because each form of treatment acts on a different part of the bacteria to disarm and destroy it, says Carlton.

Overcoming a Bad Reputation

Phage therapy has been deemed a success in parts of eastern Europe for decades. In Tbilisi, Georgia, home of the Eliava Institute of Bacteriophage, Microbiology, and Virology, where phages have been studied since 1934, researchers report that phage therapy has an 80% success rate against enterococcus infections. In Poland, doctors have had a 90% success rate against cases of [infection with] *Staphylococcus aureus, Pseudomonas aeruginosa, Klebsiella pneumoniae*, and *Escherichia coli.*

However, phage therapy has not been well received by the wider medical community. Why is, for example, the USA so reluctant to accept a therapy that has been deemed successful in eastern Europe? Inadequate scientific methodologies used by early scientists have contributed to the perception of phage therapy as a failed approach, explains Carlton. These poor methodologies have included "the failure to conduct placebo-controlled studies, to remove endotoxins from the preparations, and to reconfirm phage viability after adding sterilising agents to the preparations," he says. Such oversights have produced mixed and allegedly fatal results—in fairness to pioneering phage scientists, their era predated the discovery of phenomena such as lysogeny, which helps identify pure phage strains, and could have enhanced their research efforts.

The new generation of phage scientists have had to overcome this bad publicity and resolve some scientific issues. For example, phages' particular taste for a specific bacterial target increases pressure to have a precise diagnosis. Rapid progressive and fatal infections shorten the timeframe in which to culture and identify a strain to select the suitable phage. Scientists have addressed these points by combining different phages into one therapy. "The down side to the specificity," says Gulig, "is that all strains of a given bacterial species may not be killed by every phage. However, this can be compensated for by using a mixture of phage that collectively covers the majority, if not all, of the known strains of a disease-causing species."

Improving Phage Therapy

Another shortcoming was that, being foreign proteins, phages were cleared from the body too quickly. "Many drugs have clearance problems," says Carlton, "and that was the case with phages." This problem was addressed by a collaborative research project that involved Exponential Biotherapies, the National Institutes of Health (NIH), and the National Cancer Institute in 1996. Led by Carl Merrill, NIH chief of the laboratory of biochemical genetics, researchers developed the "serial passage" method for isolating long-circulating strains of phages.

These long-circulating phages, produced by serial passage, were significantly more effective than the wild-type phages from which they were derived, in terms of curing animals of an otherwise fatal bacteraemia. "Long-circulating phages are important as therapeutic agents," suggests Carlton, "because the wild-type strains tend to be cleared so rapidly that they do not have time to reach and kill the infecting bacteria."

Such research breakthroughs, and data from several clinical trials presented at [the May 2000] annual meeting of the American Society for Microbiology, have won phage therapy acceptance by suggesting that it could tackle various antibiotic-resistant bacteria. For example, University of Florida researchers examined bacteriophages isolated from seawater, which could infect *Vibrio vulnificus*, which can cause serious septicemia. When they treated mice with iron overload and infected them with *V. vulnificus*, the untreated rodents died within 24 hours, compared with the phage treated mice, which recovered.

Research will continue in the hope of undoing phage therapy's poor reputation and of perfecting natural phages to make them more potent and adaptive. Although phage injections or a prescription for phage pills may still be a long way off, hospitals may be ready to benefit from this antimicrobial aid. Phages could be used in hospitals as a prophylactic to decolonise immunocompromised patients or patients waiting for surgery.

Mike DuBow (McGill University, Montreal, Canada) suggests that "phage therapy won't be a total replacement of the antibiotic arsenal but a supplement to it. But antibiotics remain too important, too successful, and too necessary to completely do without." The next stage, he believes, is more regulatory than science. "What we think we know about phages has to be verified and then deemed reproducible, safe and effective," says DuBow.

GLOSSARY

abscess: A swollen, inflamed area on the body, usually containing pus, produced by a local infection.

aerobic: Able to live or grow only where free oxygen is present.

agar: A jellylike substance made from seaweed, used as a culture medium on which to grow colonies of some types of bacteria in the laboratory.

anaerobic: Able to live or grow only where free oxygen is absent.

antibacterial: A substance that kills or stops the growth of bacteria but not necessarily other microorganisms, especially one that is used in household products rather than being taken into the body as a drug.

antibody: A substance produced by certain cells of the immune system that attaches to particular microorganisms or other foreign materials that invade the body, marking them for destruction by the immune system.

antiseptic: A substance applied to the skin or outer tissues of the body for the purpose of preventing infection by killing or stopping the growth of microorganisms; (adj.) pertaining to the prevention of infection by use of antiseptics.

asepsis: An approach to preventing infection that focuses on keeping areas free from disease-causing microorganisms rather than killing the microbes once they are there (antisepsis).

carbuncle: A painful infection under the skin consisting of a network of pus-filled boils, usually caused by the bacterium *Staphylococcus aureus.*

catheter: A hollow tube inserted into an opening in the body for the purpose of passing fluids or for other medical uses.

chemotherapy: Treating or preventing illness by means of drugs.

clinical: Having to do with the direct treatment and observation of sick people, as opposed to work done in a laboratory.

compound fracture: A bone fracture in which part of the broken bone sticks out through the skin, creating an open wound.

conjugation: A sexlike process in which microorganisms exchange genetic material.

controls: People or animals in an experiment who are not given the substance or treatment being tested; they are compared with others who receive the treatment.

contused: Bruised or otherwise injured without a break in the skin.

corpuscle: Any microscopic body, particularly a blood cell.

course of treatment: A complete series of treatment steps recommended by a doctor; for instance, taking a medication twice a day every day for two weeks.

cross-resistance: A situation in which acquisition of resistance to a particular drug results in development of resistance to the whole group of related drugs from which the drug in question comes.

culture: A growth of microorganisms or cells in a nourishing liquid or solid.

disinfectant: A substance used on nonliving surfaces such as counters or floors to kill or stop the growth of microorganisms and prevent infection.

endemic disease: A disease that is constantly present in a region at a fairly steady level.

endotoxin: A poisonous substance made by certain bacteria within the body during infections.

enterococcus: A type of bacteria that normally lives harmlessly in the digestive tract but can cause illness if it reaches other parts of the body; it is a common cause of infections in hospitalized patients.

enzyme: One of many kinds of proteins, made by cells, that help chemical reactions occur in the body.

fermentation: The breakdown of complex molecules in organic material, usually by bacteria.

genomics: The branch of science that studies the genome (an organism's complete collection of genes) as a whole.

genotypic: Determined by an organism's genes (hereditary material).

gram-negative, gram-positive: Two groups into which all bacteria can be divided, determined by their reaction to a type of stain developed by Danish microbiologist Hans Christian Gram in 1884.

granulation: The formation of tiny red granules on the surface of a wound, part of the normal healing process.

horizontal gene transfer: A process by which bacteria, even those that are not closely related, can exchange genes.

hormone: A protein made by cells in one part or organ of the body that is carried by blood or other fluids to other parts of the body and affects their action.

infectious disease: A disease caused by microorganisms.

intravenous: Into a vein or veins.

in vitro: Literally, "in glass," in the test tube, as opposed to inside a living body.

in vivo: Inside a living body.

lyse: To break down or destroy a cell, usually by destroying the cell wall.

medium: A solid or liquid material used in laboratory cultures to provide microorganisms or cells with support and nutrients.

molecular biology: The study of the composition, properties, and behavior of molecules in living cells.

morbid: Related to disease; diseased.

moribund: Close to death.

mycologist: A scientist who studies fungi.

operon: A cluster of genes that have related functions, work as a unit, and are controlled by a single regulatory gene.

otitis media: Infection or inflammation of the middle ear, a common condition in children.

pathogenic: Disease-producing.

petri dish: A round, flat glass or plastic plate with a shallow vertical rim, used to contain some types of laboratory cultures.

phenotypic: Determined by an organism's physical characteristics, which are determined by both heredity and environment.

placebo: An inactive substance often given (without the knowledge of the patient and often the test evaluator) in place of a drug during clinical testing; the reactions of patients receiving the placebo are compared with the reactions of patients receiving the actual drug.

plasmid: A small, ring-shaped genetic element, containing only a few genes, that exists outside the main genome in some bacteria; genes that confer resistance to antibiotics are often contained in plasmids, and bacteria can exchange plasmids easily.

plasticity: The ability to change easily.

prophylactic: Preventing or guarding against disease.

protocol: A formal set of rules and procedures for an experiment or treatment.

putrefaction: Breakdown, rotting, or decay of material from animals, caused by bacteria or other microorganisms.

pyemia: The presence of pus-producing bacteria in the bloodstream; a sign of a serious infection.

quinine: A drug, originally made from the bark of a South American tree (cinchona), that destroys the parasites that cause malaria; it was probably the first specific drug treatment for a disease caused by microorganisms.

sepsis: A bodywide infection due to disease-causing microorganisms in the bloodstream; sometimes called blood poisoning or septicemia.

septic: Causing or resulting from sepsis; infected or decaying due to disease-causing bacteria.

serum: The clear, watery, liquid part of the blood; sometimes, such liquid containing antibodies is given to help someone fight a particular kind of infection.

serum therapy: Treatment by injection of serums containing antibodies; this type of treatment helps a person's immune system fight an infection rather than attacking disease-causing microbes directly as antibiotics do.

shock: A condition caused by injury, blood loss, heart problems, or severe infection, marked by poor blood flow, low blood pressure, and severe effects on the body.

side-chain theory: A theory about the immune system developed by Paul Ehrlich in the early 1900s, in which he claimed that antibodies attached to antigens (substances on the surface of microorganisms or other foreign material to which the immune system reacts) by means of receptors called side chains, similar to the way that certain chemicals were thought to combine during chemical reactions.

spirochetes: A group of spiral or corkscrew-shaped microorganisms, some of which can cause serious diseases, including the sexually transmitted disease syphilis.

spontaneous generation: The (incorrect) belief that living things, such as microorganisms, can be created out of nonliving matter.

spore: A small reproductive body or cell produced by some kinds of microorganisms and simple plants, capable of maturing into a normal adult individual; in bacteria, spores are often protected from the environment and are capable of remaining inactive for a long time; they will again become active and reproduce when conditions are right.

subtherapeutic use: The use of small amounts of substances such as antibiotics to ward off disease and increase growth rather than to treat existing illness.

suppuration: The process of decay and pus production in an infected wound or sore.

systemic: Existing throughout the body or affecting the whole body.

topical: Applied only to a particular part of the body, often on the surface.

virulence: The ability to cause and spread disease; the more virulent a disease-causing microbe is, the more easily it infects living things and the more serious an illness it causes.

CHRONOLOGY

First Century B.C.

Roman poet Lucretius writes about possibility that disease is caused by invisible "seeds" that fly through the air.

1348

Black Death kills an estimated one-third to one-half of Europe's population (up to 75 million people) in one of the world's most deadly and dramatic infectious disease epidemics.

1630s

Europeans begin using bark of cinchona tree (later developed into the drug quinine) to treat malaria.

1674

Antoni van Leeuwenhoek sees "little animals" (microorganisms) with his homemade microscopes.

1860s

Louis Pasteur shows that microorganisms cause fermentation and putrefaction.

1867

Joseph Lister develops antiseptic technique for preventing infection by killing microbes in wounds.

1870s

Pasteur and others accumulate evidence supporting germ theory of disease.

1877

Pasteur determines cause of anthrax; notes that anthrax bacteria fail to cause disease when mixed with soil bacteria.

1880s

Robert Koch identifies specific types of bacteria that cause tuberculosis, cholera, and other major infectious diseases.

1889

French physician-researcher Paul Villemin coins the term "antibiosis" to describe actions by which one species harms others; the term is later used to refer to the production of chemicals that harm other species. Rudolf Emmerich and Oskar Löw begin using the antibiotic compound pyocyanase to treat patients, but its success is limited.

1905

Paul Ehrlich coins the term *magic bullet* and begins applying it to drugs.

1910

Ehrlich develops Salvarsan, the first drug designed to destroy a specific kind of microorganism in the living body.

1928

Alexander Fleming discovers penicillin.

1935

Gerhard Domagk develops the first sulfa drug.

1938

Howard Florey's group at Oxford University begins investigating penicillin.

1939

René Dubos discovers gramicidin, the first modern antibiotic to come into regular use.

1940

Florey's team shows that penicillin saves the lives of mice with streptococcus infections and begins testing it on humans.

1941

Penicillin first mass-produced in United States. Selman A. Waksman suggests that natural antibacterial substances be called "antibiotics."

1942

First mass uses of penicillin; René Dubos warns that bacteria will develop resistance to antibiotics.

1943

Selman A. Waksman discovers streptomycin.

1945

Survey reports that half the strains of *Staphylococcus aureus* are resistant to penicillin.

1947

Paul Burkholder discovers chloramphenicol (chloromycetin), the first broad-spectrum antibiotic. Benjamin Duggar discovers aureomycin (chlortetracycline).

1956

Vancomycin discovered.

1969

Attorney General William H. Stewart tells Congress that "the book will soon be closed" on infectious diseases.

1970–1990

Concern about antibiotic resistance begins to increase; few new types of antibiotics are developed. First multidrug-resistant *Staphylococcus aureus* strains appear.

1990s

Resistance to antibiotics becomes widespread.

1999

FDA approves synercid, first of a new group of antibiotics called streptogramins to be used in humans.

2000

Zyvox (linezolid), another new antibiotic, approved.

2002

First example of vancomycin-resistant *Staphylococcus aureus* reported.

Books

Sebastian G.B. Amyes, *Magic Bullets, Lost Horizons: The Rise and Fall of Antibiotics.* New York: Taylor & Francis, 2001.

Ernst Bäumler, *Paul Ehrlich: Scientist for Life.* New York: Holmes and Meier, 1984.

Lennard Bickel, *Howard Florey: The Man Who Made Penicillin.* Carlton South, Victoria, Australia: Melbourne University Press, 1995.

Nancy Day, *Killer Superbugs: The Story of Drug-Resistant Diseases.* Berkeley Heights, NJ: Enslow, 2001.

Patrice Debré, *Louis Pasteur.* Baltimore: Johns Hopkins University Press, 1998.

Paul W. Ewald, *Evolution of Infectious Disease.* New York: Oxford University Press, 1994.

Gladys L. Hobby, *Penicillin: Meeting the Challenge.* New Haven, CT: Yale University Press, 1985.

Cindy L.A. Jones, *The Antibiotic Alternative: The Natural Guide to Fighting Infection and Maintaining a Healthy Immune System.* Rochester, VT: Healing Arts, 2000.

Stuart B. Levy, *The Antibiotic Paradox: How the Misuse of Antibiotics Destroys Their Curative Powers.* 2nd ed. Cambridge, MA: Perseus Books, 2002.

André Maurois, *The Life of Sir Alexander Fleming.* New York: E.P. Dutton, 1959.

Carol L. Moberg and Zanvil A. Cohn, eds., *Launching the Antibiotic Era: Personal Accounts of the Discovery and Use of the First Antibiotics.* New York: Rockefeller University Press, 1990.

Andrew Nikiforuk, *The Fourth Horseman: A Short History of Epidemics, Plagues, and Other Scourges.* London: Phoenix, 1993.

Michael Shnayerson and Mark J. Plotkin, *The Killers Within: The Deadly Rise of Drug-Resistant Bacteria.* Boston: Little, Brown, 2003.

Kimberly M. Thompson, *Overkill.* Emmaus, PA: Rodale, 2002.

Selman A. Waksman, *My Life with the Microbes.* New York: Simon and Schuster, 1954.

Charles-Edward Amory Winslow, *The Conquest of Epidemic Disease: A Chapter in the History of Ideas.* Madison: University of Wisconsin Press, 1980.

Periodicals

Brenda Adderly, "Life Begets Life: A Closer Look at the Tiny Bacteria That Do a Big Job," *Better Nutrition*, March 2002.

Paul Barrow, "An Antibiotic Alternative?" *Chemistry and Industry*, July 24, 2000.

Clinical Infectious Diseases, "Policy Recommendations," June 1, 2002.

Consultant, "Antimicrobial Drug Resistance: Is There an Answer?" May 1999.

Consumer Reports, "Of Birds and Bacteria," January 2003.

Current Biography Yearbook, "Domagk, Gerhard (Johannes Paul)," New York: H.W. Wilson, 1958.

Madeline Drexler, "Can You Still Trust Antibiotics?" *Good Housekeeping*, December 2001.

Suzanne Gerber, "Sick Food: You Can No Longer Ignore the Problem," *Natural Health*, May/June 2002.

Laura Gilcrest, "Bacteria's Ability to Share Genes in the Body at Center of Resistance Debate," *Food Chemical News*, January 27, 2003.

———, "IOM: FDA Should Ban Use of Human Antibiotics to Promote Growth in Animals," *Food Chemical News*, March 31, 2003.

Josie Glausiusz, "The Frog Solution," *Discover*, November 1998.

Christine Gorman, David Bjerklie, and Alice Park, "Playing Chicken with Our Antibiotics," *Time*, January 21, 2002.

Harvard Health Letter, "Overdoing Antibiotics," November 2002.

Thomas Hayden, "Infectious Arms Race," *U.S. News & World Report*, December 17, 2001.

Steve Heilig, Philip Lee, and Lester Breslow, "Curtailing Antibiotic Use in Agriculture," *Western Journal of Medicine*, January 2002.

Beatrice Trum Hunter, "Uncertainties and Concerns: Animal Drugs and Microbial Resistance," *Consumers' Research Magazine*, December 2001.

Inside R&D, "New Generation of Antibiotics Is on the Way," August 1, 2001.

Michelle Meyer, "Antibiotic Resistance," *Better Homes and Gardens*, March 2001.

Christine Miot, "Antidotes for Antibiotic Use on the Farm," *BioScience*, November 2000.

Kathleen O'Neil, "Animals on Drugs," *E*, November 2000.

Peter Radetsky, "Last Days of the Wonder Drugs," *Discover*, November 1998.

Gilbert Shama, "Kulturkampf: The German Quest for Penicillin," *History Today*, March 2003.

Alexandre Spatuzza, "Are We Killing the Cures?" *Perspectives in Health Magazine*, vol. 7, no. 1, 2002.

Tufts University Health and Nutrition Letter, "Antibiotics Used in Farm Animals Causing Hard-to-Treat Infections in Humans," November 2001.

Julie Wakefield, "The Return of the Phage," *Smithsonian*, October 2000.

Densie Webb, "Antibiotic Use in Animals Leaves People Vulnerable to 'Superbugs,'" *Environmental Nutrition*, August 2002.

Kira Weissman, "Designer Drugs from Designer Bugs," *Chemistry and Industry*, July 6, 1998.

Jennifer Fisher Wilson, "Renewing the Fight Against Bacteria: Scientists Are Trying to Re-harness the Power of Antibiotics," *Scientist* March 4, 2002.

———, "Retracing Steps to Find New Antibiotics," *Scientist*, March 4, 2002.

Internet Sources

Susanna E. Bass et al., "Antibiotic Resistance," 2001. www.molbio.princeton.edu/courses/mb427/2001/projects/02/index.htm.

World Health Organization, "Global Principles for the Containment of Antimicrobial Resistance in Animals Intended for Food," 2001. www.who.int.eme/diseases/zoo/who_global_principles.html.

———, "WHO Global Strategy for Containment of Antimicrobial Resistance," 2001. www.who.int/csr/resources/publications/drugresist/EGlobal_Strat.pdf.

Web Sites

Alliance for the Prudent Use of Antibiotics, www.tufts.edu/med/apua. This nonprofit international organization, affiliated with Tufts University in Boston, works to find ways to use antibiotics that will minimize bacterial resistance to the drugs. Its Web site offers information for consumers, patients, health care practitioners, and researchers, including a discussion of the effects of antibiotic use in food animals.

Animal Health Institute, www.ahi.org. The Web site of this trade organization for manufacturers of drugs for animals claims that using antibiotics in animals raised for food helps to protect the safety of the food supply and causes minimal risk to the environment and to human health.

Centers for Disease Control and Prevention (CDC), www.cdc.gov. This Web site answers frequently asked questions about antibiotic resistance, suggests ways that patients/consumers can minimize resistance, describes the CDC's action plan to combat resistance, and more.

Florey Home Page, www.tallpoppies.net.au/florey. The Web site is devoted to biographical material about Australian-born scientist Howard Florey and his work in making penicillin into a practical drug.

Keep Antibiotics Working, www.keepantibioticsworking.com. This organization opposes overuse of antibiotics in humans and animals because it encourages development of drug-resistant microorganisms. Its Web site explains the group's reasoning and includes news stories on the issue.

INDEX